Richard:

Lots of success!

Scott R Warren

SCHEMES

&

SCAMS

SCHEMES
&
SCAMS

SCOTT WARREN

Schemes & Scams

Copyright © 2017 Scott Warren.
All rights reserved.

Published by AuthorSource
San Diego, CA
www.authorsourcemedia.com

ISBN: 978-1-947939-12-7

Printed in the United States of America

CONTENTS

For as long as humans have been on this planet, there has always been someone who wants what someone else has, and will use any means to get it. Financial scams are as old as money itself, in whatever form it may take, from shekels to precious metals to dollars to bitcoins. The schemes and scams take on many looks and feels, but all have the same basic premise—to part you from your hard-earned money. The schemes and scams have not really changed dramatically throughout history, as you will see in the examples in this book, nor have the types of players. The packaging evolves with changing times and technology, but the underlying story remains the same.

I have put together a collection of various schemes and scams that are both informative and fascinating. Some were selected for their historical significance, some for their entertainment value, some for contrast, and others just to show how anyone can be a victim. I hope you enjoy the stories and learn a little about what to look for to prevent yourself from becoming the next victim. It's possible that by the time you finish reading, there will be a new scheme hatched, and a new scam in town.

Before I get started, a few key definitions are in order.

Wikipedia defines a Ponzi scheme as:

A Ponzi scheme (/ˈpɒn.zi/; also a Ponzi game) is a fraudulent investment operation where the operator, an individual or organization, pays returns to its investors from new <u>capital</u> paid to the operators by new investors, rather than from profit earned through legitimate sources. Operators of Ponzi schemes usually entice new investors by offering higher returns than other investments, in the form of short-term returns that are either abnormally high or unusually consistent.

Ponzi schemes occasionally begin as legitimate businesses, until the business fails to achieve the returns expected. The business becomes a Ponzi scheme if it then continues under fraudulent terms. Whatever the initial situation, the perpetuation of the high returns requires an ever-increasing flow of money from new investors to sustain the scheme.[1]

The United States Securities and Exchange Commission (SEC) defines a Ponzi scheme as:

> A Ponzi scheme is an investment fraud that involves the payment of purported returns to existing investors from funds contributed by new investors. Ponzi scheme organizers often solicit new investors by promising to invest funds in opportunities claimed to generate high returns with little or no risk. In many Ponzi schemes, the fraudsters focus on attracting new money to make promised payments to earlier-stage investors to create the false

---

[1] https://en.wikipedia.org/wiki/Ponzi_scheme

appearance that investors are profiting from a legitimate business.[2]

An illegal pyramid scheme is defined by Websters dictionary as "...an unsustainable business model that involves promising participants payment or services, primarily for enrolling other people into the scheme rather than supplying any real investment or sale of products or services."

Illegal pyramid schemes are often disguised with useless products making it appear that the plan is about sales and not about recruitment. They are not illegal because of the shape of the recruitment tree, although this is a popular myth, they take on all shapes and sizes. The key to legality or illegality is in the method and mechanism for which commission payments are earned.

There are many other types of financial scams. Some historical examples are both colorful and informative in their structure and implementation. While reviewing these examples, you should see a pattern emerge that will help you better identify and avoid these schemes. I must caution you, as you will see in these examples, it is not easy to spot these schemes and scams, as the perpetrators are extremely cunning and talented in separating the individual from their money.

---

[2] https://www.sec.gov/fast-answers/answersponzihtm.html

ACKNOWLEDGMENT

Thank you to Stacy and Patrick for assisting me with the research.

IT'S ALL GREEK TO ME

In the Western World, the first known instance of men scamming their brethren occurred in 300 B.C. and involved a couple of Greek buddies, Hegestratos and Xenothemis. Today it would be known as insurance fraud.

At the time of Hegestratos and Xenothemis, shipping was a much riskier business than it is today. Boats sank all the time, losing both content and crew. Hegestratos and Xenothemis were a couple of resourceful businessmen who were a bit low on funds, so they came up with a plan to make some fast and lucrative money. The pair contracted to take a load of expensive corn from Syracuse (not the one in New York) to Athens. At that time, the buyer would take responsibility for any loss or damage that the cargo may have during the voyage. The pair took out a new invention called insurance on the boat, which would protect them in case of sinking or damage.

The pair, however, had no plans to ever deliver the corn, and in fact never loaded the boat. They figured they could get the money to replace the boat and keep the money from the expensive grain. The boat left Syracuse harbor empty. The plan was to scuttle it at sea and collect the insurance proceeds. Thus, almost simultaneously with the advent of insurance, insurance fraud was born. However, things did not go as planned.

Hegestratos set out to sink the ship and crew, but when the crew discovered his plan, due to the banging of tools on the hull, they grew understandably upset and took matters into their own hands. When the crew attacked him, Hegestratos jumped overboard and subsequently drowned.

Xenothemis had been hiding out during these events, not wanting to be attacked by the crew. The crew successfully sailed the boat into Athens harbor, and delivered it to the buyer, Protos. Protos went to inspect his precious cargo and discovered the boat's hold to be empty. Furious at this discovery, he demanded that Xenothemis pay for his actions. History is silent as to the final ramifications, but Xenothemis is not heard of again.

ROBBING PETER TO PAY PAUL SCAMS

What we refer to today as a Ponzi scheme was once known as a "Robbing Peter to Pay Paul" scam. Although the mechanisms of the scam have evolved over time, the basic tenets are the same today as they were a thousand years ago.

While everyone has a basic understanding of the phrase "robbing Peter to pay Paul," few people know where it originated and what it actually means. In simple form, it means to take from one source of funds and pay towards another source of funds. Then why not use the names Peter and Paul? Because there is more to the meaning, which us helps better understand the basis of one of the earliest Ponzi schemes.

Taking a look at the origin provides a better explanation. First, let's dispel the rumor of a biblical origin. While both Peter and Paul were Christian apostles, the two men were never in conflict, and more than likely had very little to steal. The best explanation of the phrase's origin comes from the next time a famous Peter and Paul were involved together, in which their interests conflicted. Prior to the Reformation of the Church of England, what is currently Westminster Abbey was known as the Abbey of St. Peter, located in the west of London. In the year 1066, the Abbey of St. Peter was the focus of political influence, while St. Paul's Cathedral in London's east end was the focus of the city's commercial trade. The conflict occurred when King Henry VIII designated the Abbey of St.

Peter to become a second cathedral with its own bishop and separate diocese. There was not enough money available for the construction and repair of both buildings, so lands that belonged to the Abbey of St. Peter were sold off and used to repair and renovate St. Paul's Cathedral.

With no modern transportation, the residents could not easily move back and forth from one end to the other. Additionally, the west and east ends of London are separated by the Thames River, making it difficult for people from one end to even know the residents at the other end of town. Given the size of London, most people would have never made the effort.

Had the selling off of lands for the benefit of the believers of one portion of city to the absolute detriment of the citizens at the other end of town be known, it would have been seen as a major intrusion and slap in the face from the king to the citizens of the west end. While this was likely done strictly for the economic benefit of King Henry VIII, and not for the direct benefit of any specific subjects, it still was seen as a slight to the political base of the west end. This was referred to as "robbing St. Peter's to pay St. Paul's," or more commonly, "robbing Peter to pay Paul." To expand the original definition, today the phrase means: "the taking of funds from one unsuspecting party to be used for the benefit of another unsuspecting party." This is the most direct definition of a modern day Ponzi scheme.

FOUNDING SCHEMERS

The first financial fraud scheme in the United States occurred less than two years after the ratification of the Constitution. The scheme went right to the top, or rather started almost at the top, with the first Secretary of the Treasury, Alexander Hamilton, in charge of the insider trading scam.

Hamilton, who was President George Washington's right hand man and trusted advisor, was a friend to wealthy New York investment bankers, including his wealthy father-in-law, Philip Schuyler. After the Revolutionary War, Schuyler and his friends stood to lose a fortune, as the newly formed country was in no position to repay debts incurred in the war. As well, individual states had their own currencies and the federal currency of Continentals was not backed by any collateral. The Continentals, which lost almost all of their value after the war, were still in circulation, but rapid inflation rendered them useless in commerce.

Hamilton privately convinced President Washington that for the best interests of the nation and his credibility with European allies, the United States must make good on all debts, including Continental debts at full value. At the same time, he disclosed this conversation to his father-in-law and his friends. All the while, the New York bankers, and Secretary of the Treasury Hamilton, kept the public thinking that the Continental debt would be defaulted on, and IOUs they currently held would be worthless.

Schuyler and his Wall Street cronies began buying up in bulk the Continental paper and IOUs at 10 percent of face value, knowing full well that the newly formed federal government was going to pay 100 percent of the value.

When the matter came before the Congress to vote on Hamilton's plan, virtually every member had been bought off with favors or Continental paper, including Thomas Jefferson, who was promised the new United States capital would be in his native Virginia. The only member of the Founding Fathers to stand up in opposition was James Madison, who insisted that this was cronyism and corruption and should not be allowed to stand. Hamilton's plan passed and his friends were made rich at the expense of the American people.

Fourteen years later, in 1804, after insulting the character of former Vice President Aaron Burr, Hamilton was challenged to a duel. He was shot by Burr and died the next day. Today his face adorns the $10 bill.

ONLY IN YOUR IMAGINATION

Scottish General Gregor MacGregor may have been the greatest fraudster of all time. His story could only exist with the power of imagination. MacGregor was an explorer at a time when civilizations throughout Europe were looking to the oceans for expansion. MacGregor sailed the seas in the early 1820s, looking for treasures. Scotland had no colonies, either settled or to settle in the future, so MacGregor gave them one.

MacGregor returned from his adventures with grandiose tales of a Central American land called Poyais. From 1821 to 1837 he sold the dream of Poyais to both the Scottish and English people. He told tales of the lush valleys full of huge trees overflowing with delectable fruits. He told of the pristine waters, so delicious to taste, and full of fish. He regaled listeners with stories of the rivers lined with gold. He also noted that the only thing missing from Poyais were settlers, and those with bravery and foresight could settle the land and flourish like none before. Poyais was the dream of the future.

MacGregor showed pictures of the land, the mountains, rivers, valleys, and ocean. These pictures painted a beautiful scene, one that any settler would love to buy into. There was just one problem with the entire story: Poyais did not exist. It was an elaborate scheme to fleece the citizens of the region.

For his efforts, MacGregor raised 1.3 million pounds through the sale of government bonds and land title grants. Since there was no country and no land, the bonds and grants were completely fraudulent, and all the money went straight into MacGregor's pockets. It would be a simple case of fraud had the story ended there—but it didn't.

Some 250 eager settlers packed their belongings onto seven ships and made the voyage to the wondrous land of Poyais. When they arrived at the set destination, all they found was unbearable, untamed jungles. Without enough supplies to return to Scotland, they had to attempt to survive. More than 200 perished, with about 50 able to make the trip back to Scotland, alive. Those who returned brought charges against MacGregor, but some of them actually defended him and placed the blame on the leaders of the emigration party. They stated that they must have landed at the wrong location, and the general was not tried.

MacGregor tried the same scheme in France a few years later, and was brought to trial for fraud. He was acquitted of all charges. He ran the same Poyais scams all over London for the greater part of the next decade and made a nice living, but was never convicted of any crime. In his 50s, he moved to Venezuela and lived out his life in luxury. He died in 1845 and was buried with full military honors.

COLD SPRINGS TRAGEDY

O ne of the earliest American examples, and quite possibly the most intriguing, is the case that became known as the Cold Springs tragedy. On September 12, 1868 in Cold Springs, Indiana, a well-known Indianapolis "broker," Jacob Young, and his wife Nancy, were murdered. While investigating the murders, an amazing history of financial events was discovered.

Mr. Young would borrow money from individuals with the promise of extraordinary returns. For some time, they would provide the lenders with the promised returns, earning their trust, all the while borrowing more and more with future promises. He had two business partners, Nancy Clem and William Abrams. Yet no one had an office and all business was conducted on the streets or in the social settings of the lenders.

It is very likely that Ms. Clem was the mastermind behind the scheme and was also the mastermind behind the murders. One early investor, a Mr. Charles Duzan of Indianapolis, made many loans, strictly through Ms. Clem, ranging from $500 to $20,000. In the span of four months, Mr. Duzan had a net gain of $9,000. Shortly after, he made a loan of $20,000 available at 25 percent interest, payable shortly thereafter.

At the same time, the trio were taking loans from all over town, with the 25 percent interest promise. Some people started to get leery and asked for their principal back, which the trio refused. The scheme was showing signs of cracking, and Mr. Young decided to get out. He knew they did not have the funds to repay Mr. Duzan. He and his wife packed up their horse and buggy, along with about $7,000, and left town. The next day, their bodies were found in Cold Springs, by the side of a river bed, face down in the mud. Mr. Young had been shot in the face, almost unidentifiable, while Mrs. Young had been shot in the head and burned from the top of her chest to her feet. Mrs. Young had also been hit in the head with a blunt object.

At first it was claimed to be a murder-suicide, but investigators soon discovered that, although a shotgun was found at the scene that matched the shots killing Mr. Young, it was too far from his body for him to have used it to kill Mrs. Young. Further investigation showed that a pistol had been used to kill Mrs. Young, and there was no pistol at the scene.

Other evidence obtained included a woman's footprint in the mud near the bodies, which did not match Mrs. Young, and distinctive horseshoe prints nearby leaving the scene. On the night of the murders, eyewitnesses reported seeing another woman getting into the buggy with the Youngs as well as a second buggy containing Mr. Abrams and a Mr. Silas Hartman, the brother of Nancy Clem. The horseshoe prints on the "Hartman" buggy matched the distinctive pattern on the prints at the scene, and the shoes of Ms. Clem perfectly matched the shoe prints found at the scene.

Although the evidence showed that Mr. Young was carrying a significant sum of money, none was found on his body. When police discovered the business connection between the Youngs and Mrs. Clem and Mr. Abrams, it was enough for them to put all the pieces together and arrest the pair, as well as Mr. Hartman.

The defendants were all tried separately, but the trial of Ms. Clem garnered most publicity, as it was uncommon to have a woman on trial for any murder, let alone such a gruesome and tangled one. Her first trial ended in a hung jury and she was retried. At her second trial, she was convicted of second degree murder; the jury could not see its way to finding a woman guilty of first degree murder. The prosecuting attorney was future United States President Benjamin Harrison. On technicalities, the conviction was overturned and she was retried a third time. It seemed that the defense continually tried to delay the third trial, in the hopes that witnesses would either move away or die off. The third trial lasted a month and ended in another hung jury. She was tried a fourth time some four years after the murders, and was convicted and sentenced to life in prison. The verdict was appealed, and was returned to the lower court to be retried for a fifth time. By this point, everybody had pretty much forgotten about the whole affair, and the state could not afford another trial, so Ms. Clem was set free.

While awaiting trial, Mr. Hartman issued a bizarre confession on the eve of his hearing. He claimed that a whole bunch of other people, who had alibis and no direct knowledge of the murders, had done it all. He knew they were going to commit murder, but took no part. Later that night, he was found hanged in his cell by his own hand.

Mr. Abrams was tried, convicted, and sentenced to life in prison for his part in the murders.

No one has ever determined what actually happened that night. During the investigation of the murders, the financial crimes were exposed. Most of the high society individuals that were scammed did not want to come forward and prosecute, due to the embarrassment of being conned, and the likely prospect that the individuals responsible would be spending the rest of their lives in a cell for murder. It is estimated that the trio ran their "Robbing Peter to

Pay Paul" scam to the tune of several hundred thousand dollars. However, based on shoddy record keeping, and the fact that neither of the surviving thieves would discuss the scam, the exact amount will never be known.

THE SCAM THAT KILLED A PRESIDENT

In 1880, a young man in his late twenties, Ferdinand Ward, started on a path that would earn him the nickname of "the best-hated man in the United States." Ward was the son of a respected Baptist minister, and he met and befriended, through their fathers, Buck Grant, the son of President Ulysses S. Grant. He convinced Buck to go into business with him, and they formed the investment brokerage house of Grant & Ward.

Based on the financial claims made and the Grant name, the investors rolled in. Ward told everyone he talked to that the firm had the backing of the president, and that he was a silent partner. In truth, there was little or no investment activity taking place. The entire operation was a scam. Ward was simply taking from new investors to make payments to old investors.

In 1883, President Grant himself invested $100,000 of personal funds into the firm. In early 1884, The president grew curious as to the investments and questioned Ward. Cool as a cucumber, Ward told Grant that the losses were only about $600,000, then calmly wrote Grant a check for $1,000,000 from a well-respected bank. The president was satisfied by the charismatic Ward, and decided not to cash the check.

President Grant proceeded immediately to his good friend, Henry Vanderbilt, and inquired about a loan to cover the short-term losses.

Vanderbilt, the richest man in America, loaned Grant $150,000, no questions asked. When Grant got home that night, he thought he was rich, only to discover two days later that the $80 in his pocket and $30 in his wife's was all they had left. To his dismay, he realized he'd been conned, and the check from Ward was worthless. The doors to Grant & Ward were closed abruptly and the firm filed bankruptcy. An arrest warrant was issued for Ferdinand Ward.

Ward was arrested, tried and sentenced to ten years of hard labor in Sing Sing prison. In total, the money stolen from investors by Ward, using the name of the Grant family, totaled $14 million. President Grant felt personally responsible and sold everything he owned, including war medals, swords, and presidential mementos in order to satisfy as much of the debt as he could. He sold whatever belongings he had of any value, but still could not pay back the loan in full. Vanderbilt, to his credit, did not hold Grant to repayment, having great respect and love for the man. However, the now ex-president was a man of pride and integrity, and insisted on paying back what he could.

In 1885, as Grant lay dying of cancer, he began dictating his memoirs, *Personal Memoirs of U.S. Grant,* with the entire proceeds to be used to pay back the loan and investors that were robbed by Ward. He died just days after completing the work. His death has been widely blamed on the stress and guilt of the Grant & Ward scam orchestrated by Ferdinand Ward.

Ward was released from Sing Sing in 1892. While in prison, his wife died, leaving a son behind, with a trust fund from his grandparents. Upon his release, Ward hired thugs to kidnap his own son with the intent of stealing his trust fund. He spent the final 32 years of his life extorting payments from his Puritan Baptist parents for the safe treatment and return of his son.

SILVER SCAM

In the early 1890s in the beautiful countryside town of Surrey, England, James Wright set up one of the earliest mining scam operations. It is clear from history that Mr. Wright may not originally have set out to run his operations as a financial scam, but events which didn't go his way led him down a criminal path.

Wright's path began in the early 1870s when he moved to Canada and began promoting silver mining operations in Canada, Colorado, and New Mexico. He was very successful in these promotions, making a small fortune in the process, although never making any profits for any of his investors.

In 1889 he returned to his native England as a newly minted millionaire, with a beautiful, young American wife in tow. Gold had recently been discovered in Australia and, with his experience in mining promotion, Wright seized on the opportunity to exploit the boom. He set up a series of companies, the British and American Corporation, the Standard Exploration Company, and the London and Globe Finance Corporation.

Wright was a genius in his planning. In order to give credibility to the companies, he placed well respected international leaders in positions on the board of directors. At the outset, he placed the High Commissioner to South Africa, the Governor-general of Canada, and Viceroy of India on the board of all the companies.

To further his credibility as a successful mining maverick, he purchased a mansion in a High Street neighborhood, the home to lords and ladies. He purchased a racing yacht and several parcels of land to create a grand estate with boathouse, theater, dancehall, and underwater viewing tunnels. Everything to build this estate was imported from throughout Europe. He was living extremely high on the hog.

The high life didn't last long, as his investments failed to flourish and investors grew tired of his lavish lifestyle at their expense. As losses mounted, Wright began to "cook the books" by providing loans from one company to the other, making each company look solvent, when in fact no money was available for the loans or repayment. The company balance sheets began to get more and more distorted and misrepresented.

Just before Christmas 1890, investor suspicions came to a head. It was announced that despite the profits and success shown on the balance sheets, there would be no annual dividend. Questions and accusations began to fly, for which Wright had no answers. Three days after Christmas, the companies all collapsed and Wright fled the country.

He had landed in Paris, then booked a luxurious suite on a vessel bound for New York under an assumed name, and with fraudulent documents. Meanwhile, the court in London was apprehensive about filing charges against Wright, probably because of his connections and the lack of adequate financial fraud laws, but the lavish spending and obvious flight convinced the judge to issue an arrest warrant.

When the ship arrived in New York, he was greeted at Ellis Island by police officers waiting to arrest him and return him to England to stand trial. Up to and throughout his trial, he maintained his innocence, claiming all the losses were the result of jealous competitors. He asserted that the money was all there and he was doing great.

Upon cross-examination in the closing days of trial, his entire case collapsed. The assets that he claimed to be worth over 7 million pounds, were proven to be worth less than 1.5 million pounds, with the rest having been spent by Wright. The prosecutor took the case and financials apart piece-by-piece and pointed out all the games Wright had been playing with the books and records. Wright grew solemn at the defense table.

The jury deliberated for a mere 45 minutes prior to convicting him on 24 counts of fraud. The judge, noting Wright's lack of remorse or responsibility, stated that he had no choice but to sentence him to seven years in prison. Remarkably, upon the news of his conviction, Wright's demeanor improved dramatically.

He was transferred into a courtroom waiting room, where he smoked a cigar with deputies while waiting for his transfer to jail. After taking a few puffs, his face began to change color, then he staggered and fell to the ground.

He was dead.

He had taken a cyanide tablet and committed suicide. A revolver with six bullets in the chamber was also found in his pocket. He obviously knew where the trial was headed, knew he was guilty, and had no intention of serving any time in prison. The autopsy showed that he had taken enough cyanide to kill several men much larger than himself. Wright had left nothing to chance. No investor would ever see their money again.

WILLIAM "520 PERCENT" MILLER

L ong before Charles Ponzi got naming credit for the "Robbing Peter to Pay Paul" scam around the world, a little-known American scammer, William Miller, came up with the model in March of 1899. Miller was a charismatic young man who grew up in Brooklyn, looking for ways to make some money. He was a Sunday school teacher and, as such, had the trust of a large group of young men whom he taught.

Along with a partner, Mr. Miller put together a "company" called the Franklin Syndicate, using the image of Benjamin Franklin in his logo to further gain credibility. Mr. Miller would take weekly trips into New York City to visit Wall Street, where he was said to have great contacts and insider information. These rumors proliferated quickly. He started out by telling the young men in his Bible study and Sunday school classes that he knew Wall Street secrets, and a $10 investment in the Syndicate would return a profit of 520 percent per year.

He followed up his promises with a written guarantee that contained a big picture of Benjamin Franklin in the middle, which stated that interest payments of $1.00 per week would be paid on a $10 investment, with the remainder paid at the end of a one-year period. It further stated that principal could be withdrawn at any point, illustrating the lack of risk in the investment. Some people were hesitant; $10 was a lot of money in 1899 for a working class person, but they were reassured when they saw friends receiving their $1.00 per week payout. It seemed like a good deal all around. When individuals saw their $1.00 per week payout, people wanted to up their investment, which Miller was happy to accommodate. More and more people put in more and more money. The scam spread throughout working class Brooklyn, to small business owners, shop workers, police, and other public servants.

At its height, Miller had an estimated 12,000 depositors bringing in over $60,000 per day. The problem? There was no Wall Street insider information, nor was there any investment. Miller and his partner were simply putting the money into their own pockets and paying out the small amounts to keep people hooked.

All in all, the scheme lasted less than a year, and came crashing down in November, 1899. Miller's partner fled to Europe, never to be seen again, but he was rumored to be conducting similar scams throughout Paris society. When he was arrested, Miller hid over $180,000 with his crooked lawyer. In May 1901, he was sentenced to ten years in prison.

Miller's lawyer pulled a scam of his own, telling Miller to hide the money with him and he would take care of Miller's young wife and baby. The lawyer provided the wife and child with a mere $10 per week, and he blackmailed Miller. If he ever spoke up about the money, the lawyer would force the young family out on the streets to starve.

In 1903, an angry and somewhat repentant Miller testified with a full confession. He also laid out the lawyer's part in the scheme, which resulted in the lawyer's conviction. Miller further assisted the District Attorney in recovery of some of the money hidden by the lawyer and returned it to investors. He was pardoned by the governor after serving six years, for his assistance in the case.

William Miller turned over a new leaf and was known the rest of his life as "Honest Bill." He moved to the small town of Rockville Center, New York, and sold groceries for the rest of his days. He lived a quiet life until he was contacted by a reporter from *New York World* magazine in 1920. The reporter wanted to question him about a new investment going around and get his thoughts on it. The investment was with a young Italian immigrant named Charles Ponzi. When asked, Mr. Miller responded, "I may be rather dense but I can't understand how Ponzi made so much money in so short a time in foreign exchange." When asked if he would like to trade place with Ponzi, he replied, "I would much rather own this grocery store, where I have few worries and breathe God's free pure country air." Miller was one of the few schemers known to have changed his ways, unlike the target of the questions, Charles Ponzi.

THE PONZI SCHEME

B orn in Italy in 1882, Carlo Ponzi came to America as a young man and economy passenger aboard the SS Vancouver in 1903. Sometime shortly after arriving in the United States, Carlo became known as Charles, the name he would carry to infamy. Broke from gambling, Ponzi had big dreams of riches. Unfortunately, he possessed little in the way of skills to achieve his riches. He worked odd jobs, until he found a job as a bank teller in Montreal, Canada, at a newly established bank catering to lending money to recent immigrants with no credit history at very high interest rates. Shortly thereafter, the bank went bankrupt when many of the loans defaulted. Ponzi was left jobless and broke in a foreign land with no family structure. He then began scheming but was caught forging checks and was sentenced to three years in a Canadian prison. While serving his sentence, he wrote letters to his family in Italy telling them that he had found a great job in the Canadian prison system.

When he finished serving his term, he returned to the United States and started on his next venture. He found a lucrative niche in the illegal immigration field, becoming a human trafficker and smuggling illegal Italian immigrants into the United States. As with most, if not all, of his other ventures, he was not very sly and was eventually caught, convicted and again sentenced to time behind bars, this time two years in an Atlanta prison. After that stint, he went into real estate, where he sold Florida underwater swamp land to out of state investors. Another stint in prison would follow.

Having wasted his twenties in prison, upon his release he spent a few years working odd jobs again all the while dreaming of vast riches. In 1920, he gained the inspiration that would give rise to the famous "naming rights" for which he will forever be known: the "Ponzi scheme." The scheme, which started out as a legitimate venture, revolved around priority airmail postage stamps. At the time, there was something called an "International Reply Coupon," which could be exchanged for Priority Airmail Postage Stamps from a different country. Ponzi realized that he could buy these stamps from one country and exchange them for stamps from another country at a profit. Ponzi devised a plan whereby he would send money to a person in one country to buy the International Reply Coupons and send them to him in the United States. He would then redeem the coupons, which were worth more in the United States than in the country of origin, and sell the stamps. Some reports say that he made as much as 400 percent return on his money. The profiteering from International Reply Coupons was not technically illegal, but it is not known if anyone had exploited this loophole in the system prior to Ponzi.

Ponzi was not satisfied with his small scale personal operation, and decided to step it up to the big stage. He began seeking investors into his plan, with promises of 100 percent profit in as little as 90 days. Soon thereafter, government bureaucracy caught on to the stamp arbitrage that was occurring and put a stop to the profitability of the venture. This didn't stop Ponzi; indeed it didn't even slow him down. He began promising higher returns and began taking in more and more money. He began the process of paying out the older investors with the funds from the newer investors and not even buying the stamps any longer.

Ponzi was making huge sums of money in a very short time. It is estimated that he was making over $250,000 a day. He was able to purchase a beautiful mansion with a swimming pool and the unheard of luxury in 1920 of indoor air conditioning. Reporters from the Boston Post began investigating this phenomenon, and were quickly followed by other publications. What they uncovered was that Ponzi was actually operating at a net loss and there were no profits to be made from the stamp trade. As the scheme began to unravel, investors demanded their money back, which of course could not be given, as it had either been used to pay back older investors (to keep them in the scheme) or spent by Ponzi. On August 12, 1920, it all came crashing down, just short of a year after it began, this time resulting in another arrest for Ponzi, charging him with 86 separate counts of mail fraud this time. At the time of his arrest, he was indebted for an estimated $7 million to thousands of individuals.

Ponzi pled guilty to all charges, and was sentenced to life in prison, of which he served 14 years. His scheme collapse cost investors an estimated $20 million and forced six local banks to fail. The newspapers of Boston and New York began referring to the whole episode as the "Ponzi Scheme," which has stood to this day.

Upon his release from prison in 1935, Ponzi left the United States, under a deportation order, and was returned to his native Italy, where he went to work for dictator Benito Mussolini. Over the next several years he tried his hand at various other scams and schemes around the world, never holding a legitimate job again. He died in Rio de Janeiro, Brazil, in 1949 without a penny to his name. On his deathbed he admitted that he had in fact intended on stealing money from unsuspecting investors all along, and bragged at how successful he had been.

KREUGER FINDS A MATCH

Almost ten years after Ponzi's scheme took place, and a continent away in Europe, came proof that not all schemes start out with a nefarious purpose. In a quiet old world Swedish town in the early 1930s, wealthy young Swedish business magnate Ivar Kreuger went from hero to villain in a few short months. Kreuger was known as the "Match King" for building a huge business empire that started with the small flicker of the simplest of inventions, the wooden Swedish safety match. In 1929, Kreuger was worth more than nine times the total amount of all bank loans in Sweden, more than $110 billion in today's money.

Kreuger's father owned two factories that produced the safety matches, which changed the manner in which the world started fires, with the simple swipe of the match on the side of the box. Young Ivan didn't think much of the "small" family business and set out to make a fortune for himself in other avenues. At the conclusion of World War 1, match use grew significantly worldwide with the introduction of gas ovens and stoves and the popularization of cigarettes. Kreuger saw this as an opportunity, and he convinced Sweden's top banks to back him in loans to take over his father's business. Kreuger's uncle also owned a match factory, and was an alcoholic, so while he was in a drunken stupor young Ivan tricked him into signing over his factory interest. He then turned these factories into "stock" companies and sold shares in each.

A match factory, of a small scale, was a reasonably easy business to start, and small factories began popping up all over Europe. These factories were not generally efficient and ran at small profit margins at best. Kreuger planned to purchase as many as possible to gain a monopoly in the industry. He borrowed money from individuals, with promises of huge returns, in order to purchase match factories, both in Europe and eventually throughout the world.

This was just the beginning for Kreuger, who realized that the world was facing dire financial situations almost at every turn. He decided that he could loan money to governments in desperate need of funds, and in exchange get the government to declare him the monopoly owner in that country, thus eliminating all competition. He loaned $125 million to Germany, $75 million to France, $10 million to Turkey, $38 million to Poland. More than a dozen other countries obtained loans from Kreuger in exchange for granting him the monopoly rights. In 1930, he planned to loan $75 million to Italy, but that deal was never officially consummated.

To finance these loans, Kreuger took investment from investors in the United States worth over $150 million. At the start of the Great Depression, spurred by the stock market crash of 1929, Kreuger's international match company stock was withstanding the crash and even growing, with monopolies or government exclusivity contracts in more than 40 countries. By 1931, Kreuger was advertising different investment opportunities to investors around the globe, with large returns secured by the government loan repayments and growth of the match empire.

Cracks began to show in the business structure, when it was realized that match production and sales was just not a very profitable business. In fact, Kreuger was using the funds from new investors to make payments to old investors and was actually losing money in the businesses. His empire grew to over $600 million dollars, and although he only controlled 1 percent of the stock at this point, he sat on top of and controlled the flow of all of the money.

Investors began asking questions, such as, "What assets does the company own?" "What does real estate assets outside of the match business refer to?" "When will we be seeing a return on investment?" However, Kreuger ignored their pleas. In fact, to close relations, he professed to being upset at being questioned. Soon he would need to come up with a $50 million payment to the investors on the German loan, and he had no way of obtaining these funds unless he found more investors. He told anyone who would listen that all assets and investments were secured by bonds from the Italian government that were safely locked in his safe. All was well.

Unbeknownst to anyone except Kreuger himself, the signatures on the Italian bonds were all forged by Kreuger, and none of the investments were secured. He must have suspected that his scam was falling apart and would soon be exposed, because on March 11, 1932, Ivar Kreuger walked into a Paris gun shop and purchased a 9mm revolver. That night, he tried to transfer valuables to family and friends. On March 12, 1932, Kreuger was found in bed with a single gunshot wound straight through his heart. While his death was declared a suicide, family members and historians opine that he may have been murdered by unhappy investors.

After his death many facts became clear. First, the "Match Empire" had been losing money for some time and that in its very best times, profit margins were so small they could not sustain or produce the returns promised and provided by Kreuger.

Second, Kreuger had the books and records so confused and incorrect that teams of accountants and government tax authorities could not decipher them. Kreuger's financial statements turned out to be fraudulent with double and triple booking of assets to make it look like the match business was highly profitable. To this day, it is not readily known how much was lost on Kreuger's scam. It took investigators over five years to try to figure out the accounts of over 400 companies set up by Kreuger. The closest they could come to a conclusion was that Kreuger himself went through approximately $400 million of investor funds.

What is widely known is the impact his scam had on the financial institutions of the world, in and out of Sweden. Besides the individual hardships and tragedy caused to the investors, financial institutions failed, making the Great Depression even worse.

On the positive side, the Kreuger scam, which started as a legitimate attempt to consolidate an industry, shed light on the governments of the world that oversight was lacking on investment opportunities. In the United States, this led directly to the enactment of the Securities Act of 1933, which strengthened the disclosure requirements for any company selling stock, as well as other additional protections. These laws are still in full force today.

SOMETHING SMELLS ROTTEN

In 1984, in South Africa, a scam began that took the country by storm and became known as the Rotten Milk Scam. It was started by a middle aged man named Adriaan Nieuwoudt, who claimed to have gained the inspiration for the company from his grandmother. He claimed to have come up with a powdery substance that, when mixed with milk and graded cheese, would produce a culture that could be used to make life altering skincare products. He sold the powder, called "activator kits," to distributors, for 500 rand (today about $36). The distributor would then add the milk and cheese and wait for the culture to grow. They would then dry out the culture and skim off the top layer, and place it in an envelope and return it to the company, which in turn would pay them 100 rand. Each culture took a week to ferment. After five returns, the distributor would break even and the rest would be profit. It was said that each batch could make 15 cultures, thus creating a 150 percent profit for the distributor. The cultures returned to the company would then be used to make awesome skincare products.

The reality was quite different. The returned envelopes were simply emptied out, and sent right back out as new "activator kits." There were no actual skincare products. The fallacy that each culture could make 15 batches before losing its efficacy was clear: batch after batch came from the same original powder. The scheme took in 140 million rand before authorities shut it down. In an ironic twist, when shutting down the company, authorities alleged it was an illegal lottery that was selling the chance to make money from the cultures being made into skincare products. However, when they started digging into the facts, they realized that there were in fact no skincare products and that Nieuwoudt was simply running an illegal pyramid scheme. Investigators found tons of dried culture sitting in an old shed, rotting away. Amazingly, Nieuwoudt avoided prison for this scam, but fate would catch up to him a few years later. His next scam, a diamond theft and illegal diamond trading, would land him eight years in a South African jail. He only served one year of the term, before being granted early release and starting and participating in several other schemes.

The Kubus scheme didn't end there, as one would have thought. Several aspiring scammers in the Western United States took the idea and ran with it. In 1985, a company called Activator Supply was started to create cosmetics. Another entity, Premiere Concepts was formed to market the activator kits and ferment the cultures. Another, Cleopatra's Secret, was formed to market and sell the cosmetics, which were to be made from the cultures returned. Many other entities were also formed to hide the actual operations of the scheme.

The activator kits were sold in blocks of ten for $35 each, or a $350 investment. A $6 per fermented culture returned was promised, up to one per week for 15 weeks. This would add up to $90 per kit, or a return on investment of 250 percent. It is estimated that over 27,000 people bought the kits.

The company brought in a total of $80 million before it was shut down after a few short months. There were never actually any products produced, ordered, or in development at Cleopatra's Secret, nor was there ever any intended use for the cultures returned. Investigators were satisfied that this was simply a replica of the South African Kubus scheme. Twelve individuals were indicted and

29

convicted in this case. In 1991, six years later, some investors received refunds of 21.7 cents on the dollar invested. In 1999, 15 years after the scam, civil settlement was reached with one of the individuals.

THE SPY WHO SCAMMED ME

In 1977, Ronald Rewald moved to Honolulu, Hawaii, and started an investment firm, Bishop, Baldwin, Rewald, Dillingham and Wong. Three of the "partners" of the firm, Bishop, Baldwin and Dillingham, did not exist; they were just names that Rewald pulled from newspapers regarding old high society Hawaiian families. Wong does not appear to have been a part of the scam, but was a named partner with some knowledge. Rewalt also claimed to be a lawyer with a law degree from Marquette University, which was completely fabricated.

Mr. Rewald's was a typical financial scam; he promised a 26 percent annual return on investment on funds that were invested with him. He claimed that all funds invested with his firm were guaranteed by the Federal Deposit Insurance Corporation (FDIC), which was also untrue. Rewald was tried on 98 counts of fraud and tax evasion. He stole more than $22 million from investors. He was spending over $250,000 per month on a lavish lifestyle, including the Honolulu Polo Club, horses, fleets of luxury vehicles, sporting events, first class travel, and household help. He paid for all of his luxury expenses in cash. What makes Rewald an interesting study is the back story behind his scam. He built up an elaborate life story that was mostly fabricated, but some elements of it are shrouded in intrigue and mystery.

Besides the made-up partners of his business, which were obviously names used to gain credibility, Rewald would tell anyone who listened at his securities fraud trial that his business was set up and funded by the CIA. He contended that he was a "covert" agent and that the CIA had in fact set up and funded his operation as a front to spying and intelligence gathering activities. The CIA denied any involvement at first, other than the fact that agents had been duped into investing with him. Later the CIA admitted some involvement with Rewalt, which heightened the intrigue.

Upon moving to Hawaii and setting up the firm, Rewalt appears to have walked into the Honolulu CIA offices, introduced himself, and offered to assist in any intelligence gathering needs of the agency. The CIA admitted at trial that they often use legitimate companies to provide cover for agents to assist them with concealment of their identities while travelling or working surveillance. The illusion that CIA agents are employees of a real business helps the agents gather intelligence, by providing them a back story and payroll records. Agents are given business cards and are named on stationery from the businesses, and Rewalt's firm was one such business.

The agent that recommended using Rewalt's firm did not require the normal due diligence. Thus, no one discovered the bogus partners, or many other items of interest. He concluded that he did not wish to conduct a full investigation because doing so might create curiosity and publicity from neighbors and the community. The agent wrote in his report that Rewalt was an upstanding citizen, a former NFL player, a world class sprinter, friend of Elvis Presley and several Hollywood celebrities. He wrote that Rewalt was a devout Christian with strong ties to his church and an incredibly successful businessman. At Rewalt's trial, when the agent was asked how he knew these things, he simply answered that Rewalt had told him. None of them turned out to be true.

Rewalt used his "cover" company position to entice CIA agents and high ranking military officers to invest with him. He even convinced agents to solicit other agents' investments for him. He claimed to be one of them, going as far in his trial as to claim that he was a loyal CIA patriot whose country was turning its back on him. He claimed that he was simply doing the bidding of the CIA and meant no harm. This, of course, was also untrue and part of the elaborate fantasy he had created. Rewalt represented to the agent investors that his business was simply a front for the CIA and that what it did was fund CIA operations. He alleged that the United States government was behind all his activities, convincing them that they were backed by government funds and they were playing with the "big boys," and the government would insure that they all made money.

Fortunately, Rewalt had a neighbor that worked for the IRS, who became curious about Rewalt when his children reported to him that Rewalt's children would come and go at times in chauffeured limousines. He did a little checking and found that Rewalt had shown zero income for the past two years. An investigation was opened, which at the CIA's request was temporarily halted to save them embarrassment. When the investigation reconvened, Rewalt slit his wrists in a hotel room with a suicide note next to his bed. He survived and was arrested upon release from the hospital.

As the investigation continued, IRS agents checked Rewalt's bank accounts for the missing/invested $22 million. Only $300,000 was found and recovered from the accounts. It was claimed in bankruptcy records that $2 million in assets were recovered. Wong agreed to cooperate with authorities and received a two-year sentence for his part in the firm, though he had little or no knowledge of the scheme.

After an 11-week trial in 1985, Rewald was convicted and sentenced to 80 years in prison. In 1995, after having served just ten years, he was granted parole and released. He suffered a back injury in prison that left him wheelchair bound. He is currently a talent agent in Los Angeles.

OLD MISS WHITE

In 1970, in the Portuguese village of Alvalade, at the age of 68, Maria Branca dos Santos, decided to open a bank. Ms. Branca was a poor woman without the means for such a grand gesture, but hers would be a bank like no other. She became known throughout the region as "The People's Banker," as the working poor from throughout Portugal made the trek to deposit money in the Branca bank. The bank promised returns on investment of 10 percent per month, an incredible amount for the period, and indeed for any time. Mrs. Branca became known as "Dona," not because she changed her name or went by a pseudonym, but because it was the female version of a sign of respect for criminal syndicate leaders like mob bosses.

Here is the way the scheme worked. Person "A" would make a deposit at the bank on day one; on day two Person "B" would deposit a similar amount and 10 percent would be paid to Person "A" as interest for the month; Person "B" would then be in line for "interest" payments when Person "C" deposited. When seeing the return from the "interest" payments, instead of making withdrawals, investors would make further deposits, believing in the "system" put into place by Ms. Branca.

The lines to deposit at the bank became so long, that the Dona found it necessary to open an office in the capital city of Lisbon, and later in cities throughout the country. She hired family members and close friends to work the new offices. Many of the family and friends were unsavory sorts with criminal pasts. The nature of the new "employees" gained the attention of the national police who opened an investigation.

1983, after more than a decade, in one of the longest running Ponzi schemes in history, an article was written in a national publication regarding the success of the bank. This led to tremendous increases in deposits, and also in the amount of judicial scrutiny. The Minister of Finance put out a television warning about the nature of the investment, which caused a run on the bank for withdrawals of the investors' money. The bank offices had rooms full of money with which to satisfy the deposits, at least for the short run, but the "new employees" decided to walk off with the money for their own nefarious purposes.

Mrs. Branca began writing bad checks in order to return the money, which caused prosecutors to issue a warrant for her arrest. The bank went bankrupt and finally in 1988, Ms. Branca and 68 co-defendants were arrested and sent to trial. Mrs. Branca was sentenced to ten years in prison, but served only a short portion of her term, as she was old and feeble at the time. She lived out her remaining months in a dingy home for the senile and blind. After all the years of "helping" the little guy, she died alone and only five people were at her funeral.

The intriguing story of the little old lady who ran a national Ponzi scheme for over a decade captivated the world to the point that a book, screenplay, and theatrical play have been written about her, called "A Banqueira do Povo" or "The People's Banker." The play was screened at the Portuguese National Opera in 1993.

I n 1979, in sunny sleepy San Diego, Jerry Dominelli founded the
company, J. David & company. J. David was purported to be a
foreign currency trading exchange, based on Dominelli's "expertise"
and "incredible skill" in dealing with the forex markets. Dominelli
promised returns of a minimum of 3 percent per month and upwards of 40 percent per year. At first, people he approached were
skeptical and did not invest, but events changed that made investing
with J. David seem like a no brainer.

Dominelli met Nancy Hoover, the epitome of the California girl.
She was not only attractive, athletic and smart, she was also very
involved in local politics. She was on the city council of the nearby
famous beach town of Del Mar, and in that capacity took turns as
the mayor of Del Mar. They both left their spouses and moved in
together, and Ms. Hoover became a partner at J. David & company.
With his alleged knowledge of the markets and her charisma, the
investments soon began pouring into the coffers.

Dominelli and Hoover were smart, and as money starting pouring
in, they invested back into the fabric of San Diego high society. They
donated to numerous charities, including the San Diego Opera, the
University of California San Diego swimming pool and theater, the
Balboa Aerospace Museum, and numerous political organizations
and events. One such political donation was in the promotion and
support of up-and-comer and potential future San Diego mayor,

Roger Hedgecock. Hedgcock, a young Republican (although San Diego city elections are non-partisan) ran on a platform of "anti-Los Angeles," keeping San Diego a beachfront town and not getting too urban and developed. Hedgecock won the election with huge financial and campaign ground support from Dominelli and Hoover. (Hedgecock was forced to resign after two years in office in light of an indictment for illegal campaign finance violations involving J. David & company.)

Having the mayor of the eighth largest city in the nation gave Dominelli instant credibility. He began obtaining the elite of high society from San Diego and surrounding counties, including Orange and Los Angeles, as investors. Word spread of the incredible returns and high profile investors, and J. David opened offices in New York, Phoenix and Hong Kong. At its height, J. David employed over 270 people. It seems that both investors and employees were blindly following Dominelli and Hoover, with no questions asked.

Some investors were putting in up to $10 million, simply based on the word of other investors. He was getting investment from prominent judges, lawyers, bankers, accountants, doctors, business CEOs, politicians, and many retired successful individuals.

For their part, Dominelli and Hoover were living a very comfortable life. They threw expensive parties and purchased five homes in upscale neighborhoods, numerous luxury cars, three airplanes, an international auto racing team, and even a racehorse for racing at Del Mar. In December 1983, things took a serious turn for the worse, when the firm's checks started bouncing. Dominelli had no idea how much money he was spending, or where it was all going. He made promise after promise and told lie after lie to both investors and employees about where the money was and when it would be returned. He made up stories about banks in Austria and Switzerland, foreign banks holding funds, and Bahamian investments.

J. David was forced into involuntary bankruptcy in February 1984. Dominelli was thrown into jail by the bankruptcy judge for failure to provide documentation as to a listing of investors and the location of their funds. It was estimated at the time that he had taken in approximately $112 million (which has since been reduced to approximately $80 million). After sitting in jail for the better part of one day, Dominelli agreed to provide the information. The bankruptcy trustee flew to Europe to check on the funds in the banks there, and was informed upon arrival that they did not know what he was inquiring about; they had no record of any funds deposited in their banks from Dominelli. The trustees' evaluation of his trip was that "not one penny" of the money had been located; it was all lies. When subpoenaed to court to answer for these lies, Dominelli fled the country for the island nation of Montserrat.

The political atmosphere in Montserrat was such that many parties used it for tax evasion at the time, and the banks did not disclose information to United States authorities. However, under pressure from political opponents, the administration in power at the time had no stomach for protecting and harboring a wanted accused felon. They demanded Dominelli leave. He could find no nation that would take him in, and shortly thereafter made his way to Miami, where he was arrested by federal agents.

At the next hearing on the bankruptcy proceedings, with a heavy heart, the trustee reported to the assembled crowd of investors that he was unable to locate any of their money. It had all been spent, and there was no record of the $112 million that was supposed to be invested in forex markets at the time. Certain investors were able to recover their money, about $20 million, right before news of the collapse. It is believed they were given inside information and advance warning of the upcoming bankruptcy. Included among this group were several politicians, including Mayor Roger Hedgecock, who was virtually assured of reelection prior to these events. Hedgecock resigned, and his political career was effectively over. He currently is a talk show host on political radio.

At the first bankruptcy hearing after the return of Dominelli to San Diego—held at the largest venue available in the city, because no courtroom was big enough to hold the angry and curious crowd—Dominelli appeared looking old and tired. When he was asked the anticipated questions regarding the missing $112 million, which was why more than 400 observers (mostly investors) had come, he simply bowed his head and on six occasions uttered the same words, "I decline to answer based on my Fifth Amendment right against self-incrimination." This is the last any of the investors would hear of their money.

Dominelli was sentenced to a long prison term. In 2008, he passed away, and at no point told anyone what actually happened to the money. The probable reason is that he and Hoover spent the money and kept no records or accounting on the funds. Hoover was sentenced to ten years in prison, but only spent 30 months. Upon her release, she admitted to lying at trial, admitted to throwing cancelled checks into the fireplace, and knowingly inventing false monthly statements to defraud investors.

UNITED SCIENCES LACKS SCIENCE

1 986 saw the founding of a nutritional supplement company utilizing a network marketing compensation structure called United Sciences of America (USA). The plan was relatively simple and legally sound, paying not for the recruitment of new members, but for the sale of products to consumers. USA touted celebrity spokespeople, including William Shatner, tennis star Chris Evert-Lloyd, football star Joe Montana, and baseball stars Gary Carter and Steve Garvey. USA used the celebrity spokespeople for instant credibility, USA grew rapidly and by the third quarter of 1986 claimed over 100,000 distributors, and sales volume approaching $150 million a year.

USA professed a highly impressive scientific advisory board consisting of 16 recognized professionals, including a Nobel Prize winner, university professors of medicine and science, chairman of notable hospitals, and expert medical doctors. This scientific advisory board gave the company unprecedented credibility.

In addition to the celebrity and scientific advisors, the company was founded by a successful Dallas businessman, and hired a president who was a former United States Assistant Attorney General. From a credibility standpoint, it was one of the greatest teams ever assembled. The future looked very bright for USA, with their projection of $1 billion in sales by 1989 well within reach.

Unfortunately for USA, the picture that was projected to the public was not a realistic or accurate depiction. In fact, most of the scientific advisory board agreed to participate based on promises of research grants of $1 million or more each. They were paid stipends of up to $20,000 each in exchange for use of their name and attendance at one meeting a year. There was no other requirement, nor did any of them have any involvement with the products of USA.

USA stated in its marketing that it had created the collective nutritional database, which contained "30,000 scientific studies covering 250,000 pages of documented research. Never before has a nutritional information base so complex been assembled by a single company." The company statements made it appear as if the advisory board had input in the development and formulation of the products and studies.

The health claims made by the company and its independent distributors began to receive media attention. NBC news, and Connie Chung, did an exposé on the company that exposed the claims that the products cured cancer, prevented or cured AIDS, prevented infectious disease, cured diabetes, prevented mental disorders, and many other treatments. The NBC story also revealed income claims being made by both the company and distributors.

The news story gained the attention of both the public and the Food and Drug Administration (FDA). The FDA sent out cease and desist letters to the company, instructing them to immediately stop making the medical claims and further informing the company that the claims they had been making classified the products as drugs and not nutritional supplements. Immediately following the NBC exposé, the members of the Scientific Advisory Board began coming forward and publically stating that they had no involvement, had not endorsed the products, and had no input in any scientific studies involving the products. Some actually stated that they had informed the company that the products were not up to quality standards and did not do the things claimed. Many had either already resigned or quickly resigned at this point.

The medical claims, with the addition of the income claims, and the pressure from the public following the NBC show, led the Attorney Generals of Texas, New York, and California to start investigations into USA. On January 28, 1987, the Attorney Generals of Texas, New York, and California simultaneously filed lawsuits against the company and its officers, directors, and spokespeople for operating an illegal pyramid scheme, and for making false and misleading statement of both a financial and medical nature. At this point, October 1986, sales dried up almost immediately and USA filed for bankruptcy protection.

As the dust settled, it was discovered that there was nothing special about the products and most distributors testified that they never actually took the products, they simply paid the $100 per month for the required qualifications for downline commissions, and placed the products on a shelf in their garage or gave them away to friends in an attempt to recruit them into the opportunity. Luckily, the losses for the individuals were not great, as most did not have large investments of inventory.

FLYING HIGH

I n the late 1980s throughout the world, a scheme became the latest and greatest fad. It was called the "airplane game." No one knows where it started, but separate and distinct games popped up overnight all over the world, but mostly in the United States.

This is how the scheme worked. A person would come in as one of eight passengers on the plane (which was figurative as no real flying was occurring). Each passenger would pay a fee of $1,500 to "board the flight." Each flight had four flight attendants, two co-pilots and one pilot, who paid nothing. Each passenger would come to a secret meeting location with an envelope with 15 crisp $100 bills and hand them to the pilot. The pilot would take his $12,000 and exit the flight. The two co-pilots would be promoted to pilot of two separate flights, with the flight attendants moving up to co-pilot and the passengers moving into the crew. New passengers would be found and the activity would continue, until such time as no new passengers could be found to fund the flights and they would come crashing down.

On an average night at some of the larger meetings, hundreds of flights would take off and hundreds of thousands of dollars would change hands. Regulatory agencies and law enforcement quickly caught wind of the Airplane Game outbreak and moved to shut it down. Arrests were made in cities across America from Los Angeles to New York, with Attorney Generals offices from Florida to Texas putting out warnings to consumers and taking names of anyone caught participating. Although the Airplane Game had a short flight, many other "gifting" programs following very similar outlines have been springing up and drawing the ire of law enforcement ever since.

IVORY TOWERS

In early 1993, Steven Hoffenberg, the founder of Towers Financial Corporation, was living comfortably in his Long Island mansion, when the Securities and Exchange Commission came calling. Hoffenberg was accused of operating Towers as a huge Ponzi scheme, having stolen almost $500 million dollars from unsuspecting investors, at the time reported to be the biggest financial scam in U.S. history.

Towers Financial Corporation began in the late 1980s as a debt collection company, which would buy up unpaid loans and debt from companies for pennies on the dollar, and attempt collection. Initially, the company was extremely profitable, but the rate of growth and return was not enough to satisfy the greed of Hoffenberg. As Towers grew, Hoffenberg sought investors, for the expansion of the company, with promises of extreme rates of return. He raised money through a series of bond issues and notes. Early on, he paid returns to investors.

As Towers continued to grow, at its peak employing over 750 people with multiple offices, Hoffenberg grew more emboldened and brash. He flew around on private jets, vacationed on luxurious yachts, and made large political contributions to both Democrats and Republicans.

Around Thanksgiving of 1987, Towers made an offer to purchase struggling Pan American Airlines. Neither the airlines executives, the unions, nor the Wall Street analysts took the offer seriously.

By 1988, Towers was insolvent, but that did not slow Hoffenberg down. He began raising more and more funds, from small retirees and large pension funds. The SEC opened an investigation, and Towers settled a claim that it was selling unregistered securities. The settlement was reached out of court and received very little fanfare. Business went on as usual, until the beginning of 1993 when the pompous lifestyle and lavish spending caught the attention of the SEC.

In January 1993, Hoffenberg was bragging about his wealth and offered to bail out the struggling New York Post newspaper. When the SEC questioned the accounting methods utilized by Hoffenberg to show his wealth in order to purchase the paper, things started to unravel. While the SEC investigation was commencing, Hoffenberg used the power of the pen, and had the paper run positive articles about his wealth and the purchase, and negative articles about the investigation. The SEC was able to obtain a court order, blocking the use of any assets for the purchase of the paper, pending completion of the investigation. The potential sale collapsed, leading to the purchase of the paper by News Corp. and Rupert Murdoch, who still own it today.

After the collapse of the deal, Towers filed for bankruptcy revealing $461 million in debt and virtually no assets. This in spite of recent financial statements that showed the company to be strong and thriving, which were obviously completely bogus.

Hoffenberg settled civil charges from the SEC and agreed to repay $462.6 million in restitution, and a $1 million fine, for which the SEC acknowledged there was only roughly $6 million total available in assets. Mr. Hoffenberg was also ordered to stand criminal trial on five counts ranging from fraud to tax evasion.

In court proceedings prior to his criminal trial, Mr. Hoffenberg filed a motion to set aside his settlement based on mental incapacity. His motion was denied by the judge. At the criminal trial, Hoffenberg asked for leniency, and stated that he had accepted responsibility. He then proceeded to blame everybody he could for the crimes, including his lawyers, accountants and the court appointed trustee. He further stated that, "I can't be held accountable for securities violations, I know nothing about the laws." These comments angered the prosecutor, who found the statements "truly astonishing in their arrogance." The judge also was not sympathetic.

Hoffenberg was sentenced to 20 years in prison, of which he served 18. Upon his release, he returned to New York corporate life, seemingly involved with other convicted felons. He also has been active in political circles for both parties, including setting up a Super PAC to raise money for President Trump, which has garnered the attention of the Federal Election Commission for false and misleading statements.

COLLAPSE OF ROMANIA

One of the saddest schemes in history involved the impoverished nation of Romania and swept the country in 1993. The scheme was so large that it is estimated to have consisted of a full one-third of the entire nation's liquid reserves and more than half of the nation's annual budget. The scheme affected at least 3 million Romanian citizens or 20 percent of the total population.

The scam was known as Caritas, the Latin word for "Christian love of mankind, or charity." Understanding the magnitude of a scam is difficult to even imagine, and the lack of morality in the Caritas scam go beyond anything I have studied.

At the time, Romania was going through a difficult transition from the post-communist era to a capitalist democracy. Most of this transition was simply for show as the past communist leaders, who were under brutal dictator Nicolae Ceausescu, were still in some form of leadership position. In a country where chants of "we want bread" were only a few years past, the citizens were some of the poorest in the world. In fact, the country was in a greater state of decline than it had been under the Ceausescu regime.

In the city of Cluj, Caritas was started by Ion Stoica. The promise was that for an investment of 2,000 lei ($2), investors would receive a return on investment of 16,000 lei ($16), or 800 percent in three months. There was a restriction: No one was able to touch the funds for 90 days. The money was to be invested in other markets and nationalistic endeavors.

At the time, in cities across the nation, but especially in Cluj, there was a strong nationalist movement, namely aimed at Hungarian immigrants. Caritas played upon these sentiments and partnered with the ultra-nationalist mayor of Cluj, Gheorghe Funar. Funar ran ads in local papers touting Stoica and Caritas, while at the same time raving about the damage Hungarians were doing to society. It was argued that by investing in Caritas, you were helping poor Romanians rise above the Hungarian immigrants trying to take over the country. The local paper readership increased dramatically as did the Caritas scope and investment.

Every week the paper would include a daily section that listed the names of all the people making money in Caritas (on paper), and at its height the list was over 40 pages long. However, the only people who ever saw any profit from Caritas were the scam organizers, local politicians, organized crime members, and international arms dealers. Mayor Funar helped Stoica get the Caritas scam advertised and recommended on television, and it soon spread from the town of Cluj to the entire nation of Romania.

For the Romanian people who had an average monthly household income of the equivalent of $60, $2 was a huge investment. However, once the populous publicly saw that others were making profit, many invested more and more, selling cows and family heirlooms to get involved. To most, this behavior sounds unbelievable, but these people had just lived through almost 50 years under the Soviet and Romanian dictators, and knew nothing of business, banking, or investment. They were simple farmers and artisans for the most part, and too-good-to-be-true was speaking volumes to them.

Investors were showing up at the Cluj offices of Caritas by train, bus, horse, and even donkey cart to get involved. People would even journey for days on foot to get there, mostly peasants parting with whatever funds they could part with.

Late in 1993, rumors started circulating that Caritas was not paying out and had not been investing the funds into anything other than personal expenditures for a chosen few. The President of Romania, Ion Illiescu, held a press conference in which he stated that even the least educated citizens should have been able to see that this was a scam and avoided it. This angered the 3 million citizens that had fallen victim, who also knew that to retain power Illiescu needed the support of the nationalist party in Cluj. Romanian television began run stories accusing Caritas of being a scam. Papers throughout the country, with the exception of those in Cluj, began predicting the failure of Caritas. The local Cluj papers and television remained steadfast in their support throughout, as did Mayor Funar.

The head of the Romanian Secret Police leaked a report that he had prepared, discussing the size and scope of the scheme, and how in his opinion there was no way that it could have reached this size and magnitude had it not had support from within the national government. President Illiescu stated that the government in no way supported Caritas, but acknowledged that there may well be a national uprising, if the government stepped in to stop it.

In February 1994, Caritas stopped paying anyone and declared bankruptcy. Not a single investment had ever been made and $5 billion had vanished into thin air. The people of Romania were furious and stormed the city of Cluj for answers and vengeance. If not for the intervention by international funds and world leaders, Romania likely would have become embroiled in civil war over the Caritas scam.

For his part, Ion Stoica was sentenced in 1995 to seven years in prison for fraud. On appeal, his sentence was reduced to two years, and reduced even further by the Romanian Supreme Court to 1 ½ years, or time served, and he was released. No money was recovered and no restitution was granted.

"PATRIOT'S" GAME

I n a scheme that had it all, beginning in 1993 and ending after a six-year run in 1999, Greater Ministries was destined to fail even before it began. This Florida-based scam was set up by a group of anti-government men, Gerald Payne, Patrick Talbert, Haywood Hall, Charles Eidson, James Maher, Jonathan Strawder, and Niko Shefer. When the scheme was seized, all seven men, along with their banker, were indicted on federal charges of money laundering and mail fraud.

To look at this misadventure, one must first look to the history of the players. All of the primary players in this scheme had histories of illegal activity:

Payne was convicted of lying to a grand jury in 1979 in a fraud case.

Talbert was charged shortly before the start of Greater Ministries of 42 counts of racketeering and fraud for cheating elderly people out of over a quarter of a million dollars. He was awaiting trial. He had also been previously sued multiple times in 1994 for fraud.

Eidson was convicted in 1993 of dumping toxic waste into the bay in Tampa, Florida. He was also convicted of practicing law without a license shortly before the start of Greater Ministries.

Maher was convicted in 1985 of running a Ponzi scheme in Florida. Further in 1995, he was found to have defrauded dozens of elderly Floridians of more than $1 million. Strawder pled guilty to running a previous scam very similar to Greater Ministries called Sovereign Ministries International, which took in over $13 million. Shefer served six years in a South African prison for bank fraud. Edward Mattar, who ran the bank used by Greater Ministries, also had a long history of legal issues and had been sued many times for financial fraud and contractual breaches.

These individuals collaborated in putting together the Greater Ministries scam, which preyed on a unique and highly captive audience. The group of founders were known as the "elders." Greater Ministries audience were mainly "Patriots" who believed they were sovereign citizens of their own nation, and were not subject to the laws of the United States. The main reason for this belief is their desire to not pay taxes. The group was also highly racist, with white supremacist neo-Nazi undertones. The men frequently stated that being around blacks made them physically ill and that the Jews were the enemy of the people.

The anti-government Patriot pitch was also quite effective with the Mennonite and Amish communities, which also took a dim view of governmental involvement and taxation. These groups invested hundreds of thousands of dollars.

The elders went to "church" every week, where they rallied against the evils of minorities, the government, and "outside" society. Their solution to these evils and to get "things right with God" was to give them investment, which they called "gifts." These gifts would then be taken offshore, invested in white-owned businesses of gold mines and such, and in 17 short months the gift would be returned, doubled in value. The money was purportedly invested in a gold and platinum mine in Liberia with ore deposits worth upwards of $40 billion. The elders claimed to own interests in gold mines throughout Africa worth billions, and diamond mines in South America. They also claimed to be trading in foreign currencies with inside information. They tried to purchase legitimate banks and hotels, but those deals all fell through. With the excess profits, they promised to build homeless shelters and provide rehab programs for the needy. In fact, very little, if any, money was ever invested in any mining or other venture, and no money was every used for the needy.

The elders had almost no moral compass and no scruples. They would encourage people to give them every cent out of their bank accounts, credit cards, and if need be mortgage their home. They pleaded with investors to empty out IRA's, to humble themselves before God and reap the harvest of returns. Hotel meetings were like revivals, standing room only, raising hundreds of thousands of dollars a night.

Church elders, who brought in other investors, would get paid a cash commission of 5 percent. It is alleged that some high ranking church members made hundreds of thousands of dollars, in bags of $100 bills. The leadership group of Greater Ministries made it clear to the masses that they were not being paid for their work, it was a labor of love, and they were only being paid "gas money." In reality, gas money was 5 percent of the entire take, for each of them. In fact, the banker, Mattar, paid himself and his bank president $9 million bonuses when he sensed the end was near.

The sheer number of deposits just under the $10,000 reporting limit drew the attention of the IRS, who cooperated with state regulators to take a further look into Greater Ministries operations. In early 1998, Greater Ministries was served with cease and desist letters from California, Florida, Ohio, and Pennsylvania, which they promptly ignored. Their argument to their employees was that the state governments within the United States had no jurisdiction over them; they were a sovereign nation. Of course this argument had no merit and went nowhere. In Florida, the company simply changed its name and went about business as usual. In Pennsylvania, they did nothing to comply. They were fined $6.4 million in November 1998 for ignoring the order, ordered to do no further business within Pennsylvania or with any citizen of Pennsylvania, and faced further scrutiny.

At this point, their laundering bank was shut down by regulators and their accounts were all frozen. When the bank shut down, cracks began to show in the scheme. There was not enough money in the Ponzi scheme to continue paying out old investors, and they began issuing certificates backed up by gold and silver ore deposits in non-existent mines. In March 1999, the entire gang was rounded up and indicted for fraud and money laundering. Federal marshalls sealed their headquarters and all of its contents, froze assets of the individuals, and began searching for facts and funds.

In response, Payne began rallying the troops. He decried the government action as a sign of the "end of times," and an assault on individual liberties. Remarkably, those that he had defrauded came to his aid and the aid of others. Many volunteered to do what they could financially to help them put this all behind them and move forward.

As more and more facts began to surface, the undying support began to give way. When investors were informed that the money had never been invested as promised, they were a little angry. When it was discovered that Gerald Payne had deposited over $20 million in gas money into his wife's checking account, they became dismayed. It wasn't until court hearings, when Payne testified that in fact "no money had been invested with Greater Ministries, it had all been gifted to him," therefore he owed no one any return and that he "had never promised anyone anything," that all visible support vanished.

At trial, none of the defendants showed any remorse or accepted responsibility. They claimed their rights had been violated, including their First Amendment right to practice their religion without government interference. They were all found guilty.

Gerald Payne was sentenced to twenty-seven years, his wife as a co-conspirator was sentenced to twelve-and-a-half years. The judge had planned to be lenient on Mrs. Payne, but her lack of remorse and denouncement of the court led to her sentence being increased. Patrick Talbert was sentenced to 20 years and an additional ten years on unrelated charges. Four other defendants were sentenced to between five years and twenty years. One additional defendant pled to cooperate with prosecutors and received a thirty-month sentence.

Although it was difficult for investigators to trace the missing funds, because many early investors did receive payouts, estimates are that they took in as much as $500 million and that $170 million was lost. It is estimated that more than $70 million alone was lost by the Mennonite and Amish communities in Pennsylvania.

At the time, this was the largest Ponzi scheme in U.S. history—an infamous title that did not last long.

A COUNTRY IN CRISIS

M uch like Romania in the not-too-distant past, Albania struggled with schemes of epic proportions. While the issues in Romania were largely personal to investors, the issues in Albania were much larger, literally crushing the entire nation's economy and causing the collapse of the government, extremely violent rioting, anarchy, and many deaths.

Albania, like Romania, was a country recently emerged from communism and the dictatorship of Enver Hoxha. Albania had been under Soviet rule since the end of World War II. The country was isolated from the outside world with the exception of the Soviet Union. After the fall of the Soviet Union, tiny Albania was on its own, with no support and no infrastructure. Upon Hoxha's death in 1985, the country of just over 3,500,000 million citizens began the extremely slow process of converting to a democracy and modernization of their entire society. The conversion was undertaken by the hand-picked successor to Hoxha, Ramiz Alia. Alia saw the writing on the wall and knew that the only way for the country to survive was to relax restrictions, first on individual freedoms and then on economic issues. Although Alia favored reform, hard line communists running the bureaucratic wing of the government did not, and fought him at every step. It was not until elections of 1991, when Albania elected Ylli Bufi as prime minister, and the bureaucracy was effectively replaced, that true reform began to take place.

The starting point was essentially zero, Albania being the poorest of all countries in Europe, with almost all property and business owned by the government. Businesses were turned over as favors to private individuals with no idea how to run them. These businesses included everything from manufacturing, utilities, transportation, and factories. There was also almost no banking available for the new "businessmen" to finance their operations. Three state owned banks controlled over 90 percent of the entire financial operation of the country, and had no money to lend nor the mechanism to facilitate business loans. Private investment "companies" began to form, many with organized crime ties, to facilitate the funding needs of these new private ventures.

These private funders were typical Ponzi scheme operations, promising high rates of return for the early investors from the later investors. The plan was that the businesses would turn a profit from the funds and be able to pay out profits to all the investors. The trouble was that many of these businesses had no intention of using the money for anything other than padding their own pockets. Much of the money was siphoned out of the country, or used to purchase luxury items for the business owners. Many of the businesses were nothing more than fronts for illegal arms smuggling operations into war-torn Yugoslavia.

In December 1995, the United Nations removed sanctions against Yugoslavia, thus ending the illegal smuggling trade. This caused the bottom line for the Albania business owners to dip considerably. These businesses began to promise higher rates of return for new investments, with annual rates of return promised over 100 percent. New schemes began to pop up continually, promising higher and higher returns in order to compete, some as high as 200 percent per year.

Some of the schemes, now in the dozens, were gaining hundreds of thousands of new depositors per month. In a few months, three of the schemes/companies, Vefa, Populli, and Xhafferi had over 2 million investors between them. The promises of these ventures began to skyrocket as they fought to get new investors from the competition. Return on investment promises went as high as tripling your investment every three months or the equivalent of a 1200 percent annual return.

Investment during 1996 went as high as $1.2 billion in the schemes. The government lacked regulations or organization to deal with the growing crisis. The new government became a spectator in the events as they unfolded, although they recognized that the promises were too good to be true and could not be sustained. Unsophisticated citizens, who had never felt freedom, were selling everything they owned, including the wholesale slaughter of livestock and crops to get involved in the schemes.

When international banking organizations began to point out discrepancies in the financial transactions, the Albanian government came to the defense of the schemes. The government and the people rallied together, stating publically that the world was jealous of Albania's newfound success.

In November 1996 the first domino fell. A scheme by the name of Sude began to miss payments, new money dried up, and Sude filed bankruptcy. Other schemes soon followed, with virtually all filing for bankruptcy protection within weeks. The Bank of Albania and the Federal government stepped in to attempt to ebb the tide, but it was too little too late. By January 1997, the situation was uncontrollable.

Riots began in the streets. The government, in an attempt to save face, pointed out that many of these businesses were legitimate and had real investments. Laws were passed banning illegal pyramid schemes (which were in reality Ponzi schemes).

Albania was lost, looting was rampant, a large portion of the Army had deserted, and coup attempt rumors were heard throughout the southern portion of the country. Soon the entire government structure resigned, including the president. Borders became clogged as Albanians fearing civil war fled with just the clothes on their backs and whatever they could hold. All financial mechanisms collapsed, and production of goods virtually ceased nationwide. It is estimated that as many as 3,000 innocent Albanian citizens were killed in the rioting.

Many of the perpetrators fled the country with their newfound wealth, many simply fled to avoid prosecution, and many were jailed for their actions. As late as 2016, those responsible are still being prosecuted and jailed for these events. The latest sentencing for hiding stolen funds was in April, 2016.

These schemes encompassed more than 60 percent of the entire nation's population, and almost a full 50 percent of their entire GDP. Remarkably in only a few short years following this disaster, Albania was able to make it back to the point it was at prior to these events.

X MARKS THE SPOT

The largest fraud in Canadian history began in 1993, and litigation finally concluded in 2014. The crazy matter of Bre-X is filled with intrigue, mystery, and corruption.

To understand the Bre-X scam, you must go back to 1988, when David Walsh founded Bre-X Minerals Ltd. Walsh founded the company with the plan to mine precious metals in the Northwest Territories. The company floundered and did not show a profit. Walsh took the company public on the Alberta Stock Exchange where it listed at around .30 cents per share.

With the company going nowhere, in 1993 Walsh contacted an old friend, John Felderhof, who introduced him to Philippine geologist Michael De Guzman. The three of them discussed a property in Indonesia that had been previously mined by an Australian company, Montague, and abandoned with no prospects of gold. They decide to purchase the property at a rock bottom price and prospect it.

Upon purchase, Bre-X put out a notice to investors that the site contained 1 million ounces of gold, based on reports from their geologist, Guzman, and the stock began to show life.

In 1995, Bre-X reported that the mining operation had uncovered new deposits of approximately 2.5 million ounces of gold, or four times bigger than the largest gold mine ever discovered. The stock reached $187 per share and underwent a ten shares to one split. The stock then closed, now on the Toronto Stock Exchange, at almost $29 per share, or the presplit equivalent of $290 per share.

At the Bre-X annual meeting, Felderhof told the crowd of shareholders the amazing news that the mine held at least 30 million ounces of gold. He stated that, "I think it is 30 million plus, plus, plus." In other meetings around the same time period, Felderhof was alleged to have claimed that the mine held up to 200,000,000 ounces. The stock also went public in the United States on the NASDAQ exchange. In the first ten months after the annual meeting, 111 million shares of Bre-X stock was traded.

Bre-X seemingly got too big and powerful, and the President of Indonesia decided that he wanted a piece of the pie. He demanded that Bre-X give a share of the mining operation to a company run by his daughter, or he would remove all rights to the mine from Bre-X. The company acquiesced to a 30 percent interest. Further, Bre-X was "convinced" to give a contract for mining operations to another company owner by President Suharto's eldest son, along with a 10 percent equity interest. President Suharto also "suggested" that it would be a good idea to give a 10 percent interest to the Indonesian government. After all was said and done, Bre-X was left with a 45 percent interest in the operation.

Things then started to go wrong for Bre-X. The new partners began to undertake geological studies of the mining operation. The results they come up with were markedly different than those reported by Bre-X. They discovered gold reserves. They also brought in additional well respected large mining experts for opinions.

Mysteriously a fire broke out in the Bre-X offices and destroyed all records of mining surveys and studies. Nothing else was destroyed or missing.

The reports that came back from the experts were damning. There was no gold in the mines, nor had there ever been. The gold that was found on the ore presented by Bre-X was gold that had been scraped off of jewelry and sprinkled onto the rock. The reports stated that it was the most brazen fraud ever undertaken, so simple that a child could have figured it out.

The saga of Bre-X does not end there and gets more interesting. Two weeks prior to the report of the scam, the principals of Bre-X must have known that the facts were going to come out, and things took on a dark presence. Upon being summoned to Indonesia to explain the fraud, Guzman reportedly jumped out of a helicopter from 800 feet plunging to his death. His body was not found until four days later in the jungles below, and was identified by only one individual. It is ruled a suicide by the Indonesian authorities, although it is reported that the body was found with no hands, no feet, and the penis that had been surgically removed. The body was not identified by fingerprints (for obvious reasons) nor dental records. It is further reported that a body was missing from a nearby morgue that matched the description of the body found. The body found was quickly cremated, so that it could not be examined more extensively. Guzman was said to have been travelling with a duffel bag of cash, of at least several hundred thousand dollars, which was never recovered. At least $5 million was also reported missing at the time.

A few days after Guzman's reported death, results of the fake mines were released and the largest mining fraud in history was exposed. The stock tumbled, trading was suspended, and the company filed for bankruptcy protection. Investors lost almost $6 billion.

The Canadian authorities opened up a criminal investigation involving Walsh and Felderhof. In 1999, after a two-year investigation the case was closed, citing the lack of sufficient evidence to sustain a conviction. At this point, the case against Walsh was moot, as he had died of a brain aneurysm in 1998.

In 1999, Felderhof, the last remaining defendant, faced civil charges for false and misleading statements, fraud, and insider trading. Felderhof denied any knowledge or wrongdoing and placed the blame squarely on Guzman. The case was delayed and delayed by legal maneuverings. By 2014, the court finally dismissed all charges and Felderhof, stating that any of the $75 million that he had made in the fraud was likely spent on his lifestyle and legal fees. He continues to live comfortably in his mansion in the Cayman Islands.

$3.5 million of the $6 billion was recovered, but in the end, the judge ruled that it wasn't really enough to give back to investors, and it would be unfair to give them back such a little amount. All the funds would be forfeited to Canadian charities. All related cases in the United States were also dismissed. All in all, after 20 years, no one was ever held liable for one of the largest and most blatant frauds in the history of the entire world. Based on the abject failure of the system in this case, Canadian securities enforcement rules and procedures were dramatically upgraded in an attempt to prevent this from ever happening again.

SCAMMING GETS YOU ELECTED TO THE SENATE

MMM was a company started in 1989, in post-Soviet Russia. It was named after its founders, Sergey Mavrodi, Vyacheslav Mavrodi, and Olga Melnikova. Initially, MMM was in the business of importing office machines and computers and reselling them in the Russian marketplace. The company had a stable business and actually grew at a tough time for the Russian economy.

With privatization taking place throughout the former Soviet Union, the business environment was confusing at best. Favors were being done for former Soviet officers, and businesses that were formally government owned were turned over to individuals with no experience for just a small fraction of their value, often with an IOU that would be forgiven for kickbacks. This instability gave rise to hyperinflation, greater than the United States experienced during the Great Depression.

MMM began growing from 1989 to 1992, with an emphasis on acquisition of other companies. They acquired a bank of their own and many other subsidiary businesses.

In 1992, great change came to the Russian economy. International and national arms sales became legal, gasoline and oil were deregulated, and all manner of government industry became private.

During this period of privatization, the Russian government issued "vouchers" to each citizen that could be cashed in, invested in a cooperative pool for a business venture, or invested privately. The vouchers were the equivalent of approximately $25 per person. Most citizens had no idea how to invest, and had no faith in the Russian financial system, so they were willing to sell their vouchers for next to nothing. MMM tried to take advantage of this and purchased as many vouchers as possible for as little as possible, or in the interim, to have citizens use their vouchers to invest in MMM. They were not alone in this approach, thus defeating the goal of the Russian government to get citizens actively involved in the new economy.

These activities led to the Russian Central bank suspending payments for goods and services until such time as a workable system could be put into place. According to bureaucrats, the greatest problem facing Russia in this transition was the lack of payment of taxes by individuals and companies. In late 1992, the MMM accountants were arrested and charged with tax evasion. In early 1993, the MMM bank was forced to close its doors, and not surprising all the money disappeared and no taxes were ever paid.

In 1994, MMM reestablished itself, promising huge returns on investment, as high as 3000 percent in some cases. It gained national positive attention through massive television and radio advertisement featuring the common working Russian man, homemaker women, students, and elderly pensioners, making positive lifestyle changes because of MMM investments. Russian people were not used to seeing anything on television except government programming, with only propaganda advertised, and they had never been subject to Western advertising campaigns. MMM used tactics straight out of New York or London to get the attention of the common man, and it worked to a tee.

They gained even more national attention when MMM advertised that for one day they would pay the subway fares for all Moscovites. Subway fares had recently risen from approximately .05 cents to $2.00, so this was seen as a great gift to the Russian people. MMM had become national heroes overnight. Investment capital began to pour in. Although MMM was a classic Ponzi scheme, paying out returns to investors from the new investors' money, this was not illegal in Russia at the time.

MMM grew so fast and so big, that a one point they no longer had the ability to count the money that came in. They began a daily ritual of placing the money in unused offices and counting the investment by room, such as Room number 1 of money, Room number 2 of money, and so on. It is estimated that they were bringing in approximately 100 billion rubles a day, or the equivalent of $50 million.

In July 1994, the government had grown concerned about the activities of MMM. Since there was no regulation with regard to Ponzi schemes, the government was forced to find a different avenue of attack. The Russian government used a team of accountants to estimate the rate of investment in MMM, and the payments out to investors, to determine the company profits. From this estimate, they were able to determine the taxes that should have been paid, which were not even close to the amount paid by MMM. On July 22, 1994 the government closed the offices of MMM, seized all the assets, and issued an arrest warrant for Sergey Mavrodi for tax evasion.

Mavrodi evaded arrest for about a month, but was finally captured at a Moscow apartment in August in a fantastic Special Forces style arrest, with commando officers rappelling into the apartment with night vision and machine guns. Mavrodi then made an appearance on the balcony to the cheers of neighbors.

Mavrodi was sentenced to four-and-a-half years in prison, where his legend only grew larger. In an attempt to have his sentence commuted through governmental immunity, he ran for the National State Duma, or Congress. Through support of the people he had defrauded, and for deflecting the blame for their losses from MMM to the evil government interference, he was easily elected. Having won, he never attended a single session of the Duma, nor ever voted on anything. He simply used the election victory as a means to get out of jail. In late 1995, the Duma voted to rescind his immunity and remove him from the Duma. In 1996 he ran for president, but never got on the ballot. MMM filed for bankruptcy in 1997.

Mavrodi may have fled the country at this point, but his whereabouts were unclear. He was captured again in 2003 in Moscow and sentenced three years later on fraud charges. He again received a sentence of four-and-a-half years, but was given credit for time served and spent only a month in jail.

Many changes to the Russian system transpired as a result of the MMM matter: increased regulation of Ponzi and pyramid schemes, new securities regulations, and all new rules for the Russian stock market.

In 2015 and into 2016, throughout Africa many new versions of MMM have resurfaced. It is not clear if Mavrodi is actively involved or to what extent his involvement reaches. To date, these companies have surfaced in Nigeria, Kenya, East Africa, and South Africa. They have affected over 3,000,000 people, the greatest concentration being in Nigeria. All of the African governments have issued warnings to the citizens and have begun action to cease operations.

In 2016 another branch of MMM started in China. The Chinese government was quick to issue a ban on the company and order them to cease operations. MMM seems to continue to rise from the ashes.

DEATH BY ANTS

In the beginning of the 21st century, a series of scams began throughout China involving ant farms. The scam went like this. For 10,000 Yuan, or about $1,500 you buy a collection of ant boxes. You take care of the ants, breed them, feed them, and grow them, and every 70 days you sell back the dead ants. Every 14 months, the company gave returns on investment of 3,250 Yuan, or $450. After the fourth buyback, individuals became profitable, and their ant farms would be making money from that point on. There were special rules to follow and special ant diets to follow, somewhat like the rules in the movie "Gremlins." But the number one rule was that no one could open or look in the box at the ants. Other rules included the ants being fed water mixed with sugar and honey every day at 9 a.m. and 4 p.m. They were also to be fed cake twice a week and egg yolks every few days. The boxes sent to investors were cheap cardboard with duct tape and a small plastic window.

All of the companies involved in the ant farm business stated that the power of these special Chinese ants were amazing. Claims stated that the powder from the ground-up ants was an amazing medicine, curing everything from arthritis to cancer. The most important claim, and the one that ultimately started the downfall, was as an unprecedented aphrodisiac.

The largest company operating the ant farm scam, was the Yilishen Tianxi Group. Yilishen brought in over 1 million farmers at an average cost of 50,000 Yuan, or roughly $5,200. Yilishen was well connected politically and as such received positive media attention and government intervention. Yilishen tried to bring their product to the United States, but it was rejected by the Food and Drug Administration, which stated the product was in fact a drug and that it contained high quantities of the drug sildenafil, the active ingredient in Viagra. The FDA added that the product was not natural, but contained synthetic drugs. This was the beginning of the end of the scam for Yilishen with the Hong Kong Stock Exchange refused to list the company.

The beauty of this particular scam was in the long lead times between purchase and repayment. This allowed the Ponzi scheme to continually take in investment funds without even having the need to make initial payments. Individuals would give the company their funds, do all the work, and not see any return for over a year. No one complained of being ripped off. Yilishen took in over $385 million in investment. In December 2007, the company filed for bankruptcy. The government, fearing negative publicity, blocked all Internet communications and forbade attorneys from taking cases of victims. The government went so far as to blame thousands of angry victims who stormed the company headquarters with being agitates and malcontents. No one from Yilishen was publically punished or prosecuted.

A competitor of Yilishen, Yingkoa Donghua Trading Group, was not as politically connected and not nearly as fortunate. The company ran virtually the same program as Yilishen on a smaller scale. In 2007, prior to the bankruptcy of Yilishen, the CEO of Yingkoa was arrested for operating the scam. He was quickly tried and sentenced. The sentence for crimes against the citizens, such as fraud, is death, and the sentence which he received. It is not known if the sentence was ever carried out, but generally Chinese death sentences are upheld and carried out rather quickly.

TWO DECADE SCAM

In 1983, in Orange County, California, James Lewis started a scam that would become the longest lasting Ponzi scheme on record. Mr. Lewis did business as Financial Advisory Consultants, and ran two distinct funds: the Income Fund and the Growth Fund. The Income Fund was purportedly investing in insurance premium financing and equipment lease financing, while the Growth Fund alleged to buy distressed businesses and flip them for a profit. For twenty years, the Income Fund stated an annual return of 19 percent, while the Growth Fund did better with an annual rate of return of almost 40 percent.

Mr. Lewis ran his company as a virtually secret society, with no one being allowed to invest unless they were referred personally by one of his previous investors. Initially, Lewis only solicited investment from members of the local Mormon community, which extended throughout the LDS communities in the western United States. It is estimated that he obtained investment from over 5,000 Mormon investors and hundreds outside of the church.

There was nothing unique about his plan; it was a straight Ponzi scheme, with no money actually ever invested into anything. He simply used new investor money to continue the illusion by paying out old investor interest. Most people trusted him because of his "faith" and simply took out what they needed and reinvested even more. The total take from investors was estimated at $814 million, but it is believed that number is largely inflated because a large proportion of it was from bogus interest reports. Thus, the figure includes what people thought they had earned and not what they had actually invested.

After 20 years of successfully hiding the scam, Lewis began to run short to pay interest. He concocted a story about his funds being frozen by Homeland Security and could not satisfy any withdrawal requests. This claim raised red flags to regulators, who confirmed with Homeland Security that they had placed no such hold. Meanwhile, during this period, Lewis withdrew $3 million for himself. This was the key for the Securities and Exchange Commission who went straight to federal court and obtained numerous search warrants and an arrest warrant for Lewis.

When Lewis got wind of the warrants he fled first to Florida and then to Texas, where he was ultimately apprehended. At his trial in 2006, numerous victims of the longest running Ponzi scheme in history told stories of how they were financially ruined, having given Lewis their entire life savings and cashing in their retirement accounts as Lewis had requested. Lewis sat through the entire trial showing no remorse or emotion.

Investigators were able to find $11 million of investors' money, but admitted to a shortfall of $100 million. Lewis was sentenced to 30 years in federal prison and ordered to pay back $156 million in restitution. At the time of sentencing Lewis was 60 years old and penniless, so there is no hope of the restitution ever being paid.

TWIN CITIES BILLIONS

In a scam that garnered its credibility from the businesses that were purchased with the use of the Ponzi funds, Tom Petters founded and operated Petters Company, Inc. from 2000 to 2010.

At the time of his arrest, PCI was on record as the second biggest scheme in United States history, only surpassed by the Bernie Madoff scam. It is estimated that Petters, who was the sole owner of PCI, ran $3.65 billion through the PCI Ponzi program.

The crux of the scam was that investors would invest in PCI, which would purchase high end electronic products for resale to large box chain stores, such as Costco. Petters would forge purchase orders and fraudulent wire transfer receipts to make it look like purchases and sales were being made. No such transactions ever took place. Whenever he got into a bind, with slow investments not able to keep up with the payments to old investors, he would simply blame the non-existent retailers for being slow payers and buy himself time.

What makes PCI unique is that Petters took the stolen money and purchased well-known struggling companies at bargain prices. He soon became the owner of Fingerhut, Polaroid, and Sun Country Airlines. He used these companies, which all operated at a tax loss, to "cook the books" at PCI and to gain credibility. No one believed that the owner of businesses like an airline or icon such as Polaroid could be running a Ponzi scheme. It is estimated that almost $25 billion flowed through the various business interests controlled and owned by Petters. These purchases kept the investment money flowing like never before.

In 2008, at the start of the investigation, Petters' assistant and ex-girlfriend, Deanna Coleman was growing scared of the scam and getting caught. She decided that it was in her best interest to go to law enforcement, turn the whole thing in, and cut herself the best deal possible. Coleman agreed to wear a wiretap to the office and record all goings on. Within hours of her recording, Petters was heard bragging about how all the invoices were fraudulent, the purchases non-existent, and the wire fraud. He laughed and joked about how it was amazing how he had gotten away with it for so long. He also detailed his plans to get away with the fraud if investigators ever came around (these plans were never disclosed in court documents).

Investigators from the Internal Revenue Service and United States Postal Service conducted a raid in September 2008. Records from the PCI offices, Petters' residence, and other locations were seized, and all assets frozen. Investigators began to unravel ten years of fraudulent behavior, detailing how legitimate business was never conducted by PCI, nor was it ever intended. It had been a fraud from day one.

In order to attempt to return money to the investors, the assets of Sun Country Airlines, Polaroid, and Fingerhut were all sold, but that money was used as partial settlement for the investors in those entities. Only $6.5 million was recovered for restitution to the investors in PCI.

Five individuals were convicted as co-conspirators and received sentences from one-year home detention to eleven years in federal prison. Ms. Coleman was sentenced to prison for a year and a day in a minimum security federal camp.

At trial, Petters, who ran a Ponzi scheme for 10 years, told the jury that he was sorry, and asked for leniency. The judge and jury had none, and sentenced Petters to the longest sentence for a financial crime in Minnesota history, 50 years in prison. Petters filed an appeal from prison, but it was denied. Petters was 53 years old at the time of sentence, and is expected to spend the rest of his life behind bars.

CROOKED LAWYER LIVING LARGE

A Florida law firm with 70 attorneys was brought to ruin and disgrace by the acts of its founding partner, Scott Rothstein. He orchestrated and ran a Ponzi-scheme-type operation that stole over $1.2 billion from investors. Rothstein, the founder of the firm Rothstein, Rosenfeldt, Adler PA, ran his illegal operation for almost ten years from 2000 to 2010 before its collapse.

Rothstein was a high maintenance player who liked the finest material things in life. He lived large and spent even larger. He needed to make much more money than his firm would generate in order to satisfy his greed and gluttony. He devised a plan whereby he could sell potential sexual harassment settlements to investors, with the claim that they could buy the settlement he had negotiated or was sure to achieve, at a significant discount because the client needed the money. These settlement purchases ranged from thousands of dollars to millions of dollars. In order to convince prospective investors in the settlements, he would forge settlement documents and bank records. In some instances he would even create fake court orders with forged judges' signatures.

Most of the settlements for which he took investor money were non-existent, and the money they received back was from new investors in other fake claims. In some cases, he would actually settle a matter for which he had taken investment, but not inform the client and keep the money on both ends.

Rothstein did nothing to hide his affluence; he spent on wild parties and wilder women. He bought houses along the East Coast, and exotic cars and jewelry. He flaunted his money whenever he could, and made political contributions on his own and through dummy contributors.

When he discovered that his scheme was beginning to collapse, he sent out a strange research request to all the clerks at the firm. He wanted to know of any and all countries that had no extradition treaties with either the United States or Israel. He reported that the research was for a wealthy client who was likely facing charges for white collar crimes and needed an answer right away. His staff got back with him quickly that Morocco was the only country that met that criteria. Less than two weeks later, with ticket and duffel bag full of cash (millions of dollars) in hand, Rothstein boarded a flight to Morocco.

For some reason, he decided to return from Morocco and face trial. He attempted to use his return as cooperation, stating that he voluntarily returned and deserved a reduced sentence. He admitted his guilt and asked for leniency.

At trial, Rothstein confessed, stating, "It was ego fueled. We were rolling, you know, we were living like rock stars. There were lots of things that kept fueling that. As I'm sure you realize from looking at everything, there came a point in time when the only portion about it, which was money, was keeping the Ponzi going. We had more than enough money to fuel our lifestyles. It was the power that got ahold of us and kept pulling this forward, the more power, the more money, the more money the more power." As with many of these type of schemes, the ego of the front men and the greed continue to grow as the scam progresses.

The defense asked for a sentence of 30 years, the prosecutor requested a 40-year sentence. It was expected that the judge might split the difference. Instead, the judge stated that the things Rothstein had done were "the most egregious wrongs a licensed attorney can commit" and sentenced Rothstein to 50 years. None of the victims will see their investment returned.

BERNIE GOES BIG

The story of Bernie Madoff is one of incredible power and influence, and a web of lies that ended up being the biggest scam ever on record. In the end, Bernie Madoff admitted to losing $50 billion of investors' money, although regulators estimate the number was much larger, upwards of $65 billion, far surpassing any other previous financial scam on record.

Bernie Madoff did not start out as a Ponzi schemer; he was once a well-respected member of the Wall Street community. In 1960, Bernie Madoff founded his first investment firm, Madoff Investment Securities, which became a successful small firm. He dreamed of something bigger and he saw how automation could become a positive tool in investing, and helped to form the National Association of Securities Dealers Automated Quotations (NASDAQ). He sat on the board of the National Association of Securities Dealers (NASD), and would later become the chairman of the NASDAQ for three, one-year terms. He regularly advised the Securities and Exchange Commission (SEC) on matters relating to securities regulation. His personal clients included many large funds and Hollywood celebrities.

At times during the 1970s and 1980s, Madoff was at odds with the establishment on Wall Street. He had devised a new way of trading that relied on a small spread between the buy price and the sell price. He gained large market share by making a deal with hedge funds that he would only get paid a commission on the spread, thus increasing their margins. He was often the subject of complaints, but the SEC was satisfied that this manner of business was legal. By 1990, Madoff Securities was accounting for 9 percent of all trading on the New York Stock Exchange, and a large percentage of the NASDAQ trading.

There was another side to the Madoff business other than his trading arm of an investment advisor, which is where the Ponzi scheme came into play. It is believed the scheme began sometime in the late 1980s to early 1990s. At that time, the United States was in the throes of a recession and acquiring investors was difficult for an advisor. Once the advisor gained the investor's money, it was even harder to make a profit. Madoff began to get a lot of attention for his advisory business with his clients in a down market seeing gains around 10 percent per year. In the up markets, the clients saw the same steady rate of gain. When investors requested the taking of profits, they were promptly paid, which led more and more to invest. It was considered an honor around the New York area to be a "Madoff client," and his reputation grew to near folk hero status.

During the 1990s, an investment manager at Rampart Investment Management, Frank Casey, grew suspicious of the Madoff strategy. He wanted to see if it was a viable option for Rampart, but didn't quite understand what Madoff was doing to keep steady in up and down markets. Casey had a financial analyst member of the firm Harry Markopolos do some research and reverse engineer the Madoff trades to try to figure it all out. What Markopolos came back with was remarkable. He reported that "this is a Ponzi scheme," and analogizes that Madoff's success would be the same as "a baseball player batting .925 for ten straight years." In other words, it would be impossible to have that kind of success. Further, reverse engineering the trades was not possible because the trades couldn't be found.

Markopolos submitted his findings to the SEC, which paid lip service and declined to take any action. To the SEC, Madoff was a hardworking, well-respected market maker who had been in the upper echelon of the industry for 40 years. Markopolos did not quit, and submitted a much longer, much more detailed report to the SEC in 2005, which illustrated the Ponzi aspects of Madoff's plan. The report spelled out the "front companies" and the false reports. It also detailed how Madoff was making investments for a large hedge fund without proper disclosure. Based on this report, the SEC finally opened an investigation. The investigation was quick, lasting less than six months, ending with the conclusion from the SEC that there was no evidence of fraud and that certain disclosure documents may have been overlooked and needed to be updated.

In the third quarter of 2008, the U.S. stock markets struggled mightily and several large firms, including Lehman Brothers, collapsed. Panic set in among investors and they flocked to place their money with Madoff Securities, based on the Madoff track record.

In the fourth quarter of 2008, Madoff Securities showed the first signs of cracks in the wall. Madoff confessed to his sons that he may have a hard time meeting his obligations. He began moving money in large amounts into his personal bank account. According to FRONTLINE, at this point he advised his sons that he wanted to pay out millions of dollars in bonuses to employees long before bonuses would normally be paid out. When his sons questioned his motivation, he confessed that the whole thing was a scam, and that he was finished and was going to turn himself in to authorities. His sons proceeded to contact the FBI, and the next morning Bernie Madoff was arrested at his home. When asked by the FBI if he had an innocent explanation, Madoff simply replied, "No, it was one big lie," and went off to jail.

Madoff confessed to the almost 30 years of operating a Ponzi scheme that took in between $50-$65 billion dollars in investor money. In his prepared statement to the court he stated:

> The essence of my scheme was that I represented to clients and prospective clients who wished to open investment advisory and investment trading accounts with me that I would invest their money in shares of common stock, options, and other securities of large, well-known corporations, and upon request, would return them their profits and principal. Those representations were false because for many years up and until I was arrested on December 11, 2008, I never invested those funds in the securities, as I had promised. Instead, those funds were deposited in a bank account at Chase Manhattan Bank. When clients wished to receive the profits they believed they had earned with me or to redeem their principal, I used the money in the Chase Manhattan bank account that belonged to them or other clients to pay the requested funds... To conceal my fraud, I misrepresented to clients, employees and others, that I purchased securities for clients in overseas markets. Indeed, when the United States Securities and Exchange Commission asked me to testify as part of an investigation they were conducting about my investment advisory business, I knowingly gave false testimony under oath...Another way that I concealed my fraud was through the filing of false and misleading certified audit reports and financial statements...In more recent years, I used yet another method to conceal my fraud. I wired money between the United States and the United Kingdom to make it appear as though

there were actual securities transactions executed on behalf of my investment advisory clients.[1]

Madoff acknowledged to the judge that he knew what he was doing was wrong, stating, "As I engaged in my fraud, I knew what I was doing was wrong, indeed criminal. When I began the Ponzi scheme I believed it would end shortly and I would be able to extricate myself and my clients from the scheme." Once in, he could not extricate himself and just went deeper and deeper. He knew that the day of his arrest would eventually come and had long been ready to confess and face the consequences. It is estimated that a total of $170 billion went through the Madoff Securities investment advisory business throughout the years, with $50 billion unaccounted for at the time of his arrest. His confession statement spells out perfectly the anatomy of a Ponzi scheme.

At the time of his sentencing, Bernie Madoff was 71 years old. He was sentenced to 150 years in federal prison, the maximum sentence allowed by law. While in prison, he lost both of his sons, one to suicide brought on by the shame of his father's actions, and the other to cancer. He was not able to be with either in the end. Investigators have acknowledged that finding the missing billions of dollars will likely prove impossible. The Madoff scheme is easily the largest ever, far surpassing any other scheme in scope and dollar amount.

---

[1] http://www.npr.org/templates/story/story.php?storyId=101816470

THE SKY IS THE LIMIT

In 1998, Tulsa, Oklahoma-based Skybiz.com began selling website businesses and online training courses, which they called Web Paks, at the cost of $125 each. The courses were said to train an individual purchaser on how to do any number of things on the Internet, and set up a high quality web presence for use with any ongoing business. For $125, a person would get access to all educational materials provided. Individual purchasers were encouraged to purchase numerous Web Pak packages. Skybiz was set up utilizing a multi-level marketing compensation plan that paid members for both their own sales and the sales of those recruited into their network.

In May 2001, the FTC filed an action against Skybiz in US District Court in Oklahoma, alleging that the company was in fact operating an illegal pyramid scheme. It was alleged that the products were virtually worthless, and despite the sale of $175,000,000 worth of web packages, almost none were ever even downloaded or opened. The FTC stated that Skybiz was basically using filler product to disguise the pyramid scheme, and the only reason that anyone joined was for the prospect of earning a commission from selling worthless packages to others. This point was driven home by the fact that the company had virtually no customers for the product who were not also members participating in the commission structure.

The FTC also noted that Skybiz claimed members could earn substantial income, although over 96 percent of associates never even earned back their initial investment. The FTC claimed these associates that lost money were never disclosed to prospects, and no realistic earnings representations were ever presented.

By the time the case reached trial in 2003, Skybiz had been shut down around the world. Regulators in Ireland, Bermuda, Australia, New Zealand, the United Kingdom, Canada, and South Africa were quick to act. The company, and its principles, agreed to settle the FTC action and entered into a stipulated judgment providing for a payment of $20 million, which would be used to satisfy claims from all the affected nations. Individual defendants stipulated to a ban from multi-level marketing for life, bans from being involved in illegal pyramid schemes, and injunctions prohibiting false and misleading statements.

The case illustrated the difference between legitimate multi-level marketing and illegal pyramid schemes. It contrasted the difference between customers purchasing products for the sake and efficacy of the products and for the purchase of products simply for the sake of participation in an income opportunity. It stated that it wasn't enough for a program to simply have products, but rather illustrated that the products themselves must have value.

FACING THE MUSIC

BurnLounge was one of the hottest ideas to come out in the mid-2000s, with the opportunity for the common music lover to open their own digital music store and earn money referring music to others. Anyone could become a music store owner and customize the look and feel of their store, including which types of music or artists they would highlight. For the sale of music downloads from their site, an owner would be paid a commission of .05 cents per .99 cent download, and .50 cents per 9.99 album download. When BurnLounge burst onto the music scene, it had spokespeople such as Justin Timberlake and Shaquille O'Neal.

BurnLounge had three levels of stores available for members: the Basic, the Exclusive, and the VIP. The various levels ranged in price from $30 per year to $530 per year. Each level allowed for greater access and tools, and allowed the members to gain rewards points for music downloaded from their site by consumers. There was an optional upgrade available that allowed a member to trade rewards points for cash, which was called the Mogul program.

Promoters of the opportunity held meetings throughout the country claiming that prospects could make thousands of dollars a month, or hundreds of thousands of dollars a year as a BurnLounge Mogul. In truth, more than 94 percent of all participants lost money in the plan.

In June, 2007, the FTC filed suit against BurnLounge alleging that the company was an illegal pyramid scheme, practicing Unfair and Deceptive Trade Practices, and false and misleading income statements.

The company requested a bench trial, or a trial without a jury, to be decided by a judge. The case finally went to trial in late 2011. At trial, it was shown that 62,250 people signed up in the BurnLounge program, with an amazing 60,270 signing up for the Mogul program, or more than 95 percent of all purchasers. The company did $28.3 million in revenue, and paid out a total of $17.4 million in commissions to the Moguls. Of that sum, only a mere $500,000 was actually paid for the downloading of music, the rest was for the sale of the Mogul packages. Of the total commissions paid, two-thirds, or approximately $12 million, was paid to the top 1 percent of earners.

During the eight-day trial, upon seeing the sales data evidence, the judge incredulously stated, "If package purchases were driven by the value of the merchandise included in the package rather than by the opportunity to earn cash rewards, one would expect to see comparable numbers of distributors and non-distributors buying the same packages." This was clearly not the case in this instance.

BurnLounge lost the case on all counts, and filed an immediate appeal, an extremely rare occurrence in a multi-level marketing case. The appeal was not heard until June 2014, and the lower court ruling was unanimously upheld. The United States Court of Appeals declared that BurnLounge was an illegal pyramid scheme.

The ruling in this case illustrated that the majority of revenue must come from retail sales and not from the business opportunity. The Court of Appeals noted that the rewards for recruiting must be related to the sales to the ultimate consumer. It found that BurnLounge incentivized recruiting and had little or no emphasis on the actual sale of products.

The case also found that income claims must be both accurate and factually based. The FTC determined that any claim of income must be backed with detailed disclosures of averages, median earnings, and specific earnings numbers.

The final result was a restitution penalty of $16.9 million and a prohibition from participation in a pyramid, Ponzi, chain letter scheme, or any scheme in which compensation for recruitment is unrelated to the sale of product to customers who are not participants. This established the need for customers to be outside of the business opportunity and be legitimate end users.

HI-TECH NOT A FORTUNE

Fortune Hi-Tech Marketing (FHTM) was a pretty straightforward company, selling a wide variety of products and services through a network marketing distribution channel. Fortune Hi-Tech Marketing started business in 2001, by ex-leaders from Excel Communications. The company started with the product line of long distance and local mobile phone service, DISH Network, home security systems, and various health and wellness products.

FHTM charged $250 for an individual to sign on as a sales representative, which allowed them to earn commissions from their own sales and the sales of the sales organization that they recruited. Unlike most other network marketing companies, the product lines provided by FHTM had very low margins and the commission structure was very low throughout and adjusted very top heavy in the compensation plan. This had the effect of making a few people at the top wealthy at the expense of the others further down the line.

FHTM members used high pressure tactics to convince new recruits to purchase starter packs of products, which cost anywhere between $150 and $400. These starter pack purchases would qualify a member to receive override commissions from purchases and sales of those they recruited. The large majority of members never sold the products or services, and those that made money did so mainly through the purchases of new recruits. Most did not even do that much, with 98 percent of all members spending more than they earned on a monthly basis. Close to 90 percent of members never even made back the initial $250 they paid to join the company.

Over the years FHTM grew to over 350,000 members. Following numerous complaints from consumers and an initial lawsuit filed by the State of Montana in 2010, the company made changes to its plan in Montana and paid a fine of $1 million with no admission of wrongdoing. The Montana settlement led to a piling on of sorts with investigations opened up in Illinois, Kentucky, North Carolina, Texas, and on a federal level by the FTC.

Later in 2011, FHTM entered into a settlement with the state of Texas and paid out $1.3 million, again with no admission of wrong-doing. This suit was based on the company being an illegal pyramid scheme and making false and misleading income claims. The company proceeded with business as usual after the settlement and made no significant changes in policy or training.

All three state attorney generals from Illinois, Kentucky, and North Carolina joined in a lawsuit filed by the FTC in January, 2013 in Federal Court in Illinois. At this point it was clear that the regulators had enough of the company practices and income claims, and so no chance of future behavioral changes by FHTM. The lawsuit made specific allegations with regard to the marketing practices of FHTM. These allegations included the fact that over 98 percent of all members, who were actually making anything, made less than $15 per month and a full 88 percent did not ever make enough to cover their initial purchase, while marketing claims of $100,000 per year were commonplace. It was also alleged that over 85 percent of all money earned was from the recruitment of new members and not the sale of products. The allegations further stated that the company was using the DISH Network name without authority of DISH and in fact had no contractual relationship with DISH or the other vendors whose products they touted. The FTC complaint alleged that almost all company marketing materials and presentations were focused on the recruiting of others into the plan and showed little emphasis on the actual sale of products to consumers. The FTC alleged that FHTM was generating as much as $30 million per month in revenue.

The lawsuit against FHTM and its founders was settled in a relatively short period of time. The FTC argued that the company had created consumer losses in excess of $169 million, but that only $7.7 million could be recovered. The company agreed to turn over $7.75 million to be used for consumer refunds. The defendants also agreed to a lifetime ban from operating any network marketing companies, participating in an illegal pyramid scheme, or making any false and misleading claims in a business.

In November, 2016, the FTC mailed out checks totaling $3.7 million to some of the 350,000 members that lost money. There is no indication from the FTC where the remaining money went.

MORE HOLES THAN SWISS CHEESE

S wisscash, or Swiss Mutual Fund, as it was often referred to, was a short-lived scam that operated from 2006 to early 2007. Swisscash had no relationship or affiliation with Switzerland at all, and red flags were raised from the very beginning as to its legitimacy.

Swisscash purported to be in the business of investment in various securities, including equities, commodities, and forex trading. The company was supposedly domiciled in the Commonwealth of Dominica, although it only operated through a P.O. Box, and the registers of Dominica had no listing of its existence.

Swisscash guaranteed a return on investment of 20 percent per month, or 300 percent for the required 15 month term of investment. The company raised over $80 million, mostly from investors in Malaysia and India, although both countries had issued investment scam warnings to the citizens very early on.

The company used a network marketing compensation structure, and paid out commissions for the recruitment of new investors, operating as an illegal pyramid scheme. No money was actually ever paid out on the Ponzi aspects of the plan, but some small amount of commissions were paid out on the pyramid aspects. However, what looked like a very straightforward Ponzi scheme gained the attention of regulatory agencies throughout the world for a very different reason.

Regulators in 2006 were very keen to new rules regarding knowing the identities of customers and investors, and red flags were raised that Swisscash was laundering funds for terrorist organizations and funding various Middle Eastern terrorist cells. Malaysian authorities took the lead and shut the operation down quickly. Since the shutdown, very little has been made public regarding the investigation and where it led.

Approximately $10 million of the stolen funds were recovered, and were set to be returned to investors in 2010. There is no indication whether funds were ever actually returned to date.

HE ONLY CHEATED A BIT

In February, 2011, Trendon Shavers formed an entity that would become known as Bitcoin Savings and Trust. It would become famous as the subject of the first Federal Securites Fraud case involving cryptocurrency. Ironically, it does not appear to have started out with fraudulent intent, but as it grew it became too large to handle for Shavers and he morphed the operation into a classic Ponzi scheme.

The Bitcoin Savings and Trust (BTCST) plan started out as a simple arbitrage play involving the new and volatile world of cryptocurrency, specifically bitcoin. Webster's dictionary defines "arbitrage" as the purchase of a security, commodity, or foreign currency in one market for the purpose of immediately selling it at a higher price in another market. Investors would place their bitcoins with BTCST and BTCST would sell invested bitcoins at a high rate and rebuy them at market price. The return on investment was promised at 7 percent per week. The minimum investment was 50 bitcoin. In February, 2011, bitcoin price was .96 cents per coin and with the new and explosive nature of the market, this type of return was likely possible.

As the amount of bitcoin invested with BTCST increased, the method of arbitrage became more difficult and expensive. Shavers informed his investors that he would need to reduce the future rate of return. This announcement caused a panic and run on withdrawals, which Shaver could not meet. He began to run BTCST as a classic Ponzi scheme, using money invested by new investors to pay back older investors withdrawal requests. In August, 2012 BTCST issued a blog message that it was closing down. Eleven investors were reportedly refunded, all others were promised refunds which never materialized.

In July of 2013, the SEC filed an action against Shaver and BTCST for securities fraud relating to the operation of a Ponzi scheme. A civil case judgment of $40,000,000 in disgorgement of profits (based on the rise in bitcoin value) and $300,000 in penalties was entered in September, 2014. Criminal charges were pending. In November of 2014, Shaver pled not guilty to the criminal charges, but later changed his plea to guilty and was sentenced to 18 months in federal prison.

In the crazy cryptocurrency world, the end facts of this case are astonishing. The original value of the bitcoin raised by BTCST was worth approximately $800,000. The value at the time of his sentencing for the same bitcoin was in excess of $100 million. At the time of this writing, the value is in excess of $600,000,000.

ZEEK LACKS REWARDS

Zeek Rewards, and its partner company Zeekler.com, began in January, 2011 in Lexington, Kentucky. Zeekler.com was a penny auction site that sold items based on purchased bids in different bidding formats. Zeek Rewards was an investment vehicle that promised daily returns on investment through the performance of shared tasks. These tasks included, but were not limited to, the soliciting of new bid sales, or the selling or giving away of bids to new users to the Zeekler.com site.

Members were able to either take their rewards out in the form of cash or roll them over for compound interest. The rewards were supposed to be based on daily company profits, but in fact, had absolutely no relation to the profits of the company. The company was simply run as a Ponzi scheme, taking from the funds of new investors to pay out the old when withdrawals were taken in cash.

Zeek and Zeekler were shut down by the SEC in 2012. In the preceding months, Zeek took in a total of $162 million, and paid out $160 million, notwithstanding the substantial points being rolled over. At the time of the shutdown, Zeek had $225 million in various banks around the world and over 3 billion points unredeemed. There is no way the company could have possibly sustained the façade much longer, even if they hadn't been shut down.

Zeek in operation was not much different than other Ponzi schemes throughout history. What sets Zeek apart is the disregard for the U.S. Constitution in the handling of the case by the prosecution. Procedurally, this case is unique.

Zeek was turned over to the control of a Court Appointed Receiver to manage and dispose of assets properly. The receiver then hired his own counsel to represent the company, who agreed with government attorneys on every matter, which is typical in receivership matters. What is atypical is that the receiver then selected an attorney to represent the class of individuals that had made money with the company, calling them the "Net Winners."

The Net Winners attorney was granted permission by the court to represent each and every person that made money. The attorney was not required to have contact with the individuals that he was representing, and did not need to get their permission for representation or decisions made on their behalf. He was also allowed to make binding decisions on behalf of the individuals that were not in their best interests and not seek authority from his clients. All of these issues fly in the face of the constitutional protections of due process.

In taking it a step further, the receiver made demands of the "Net Winners" and sought final default judgments against them. The judgments were based on amounts determined, without evidential support, by the receiver himself, while at the same time shifting the burden of proof from "innocent until proven guilty" to "guilty because I say so." Again, a violation of the due process clause of the constitution.

The Zeek case is a clear example of the government flexing its economic muscle and taking advantage of the little citizen. While I understand the need for a simplified mechanism for dealing with close to 9,000 people that made money, there must be a better way than trampling on the Constitution. These are tactics that have never been used before in a court in the United States.

The owners and operators of Zeek are behind bars, likely for the rest of their lives. The case is still five years post shutdown, dragging through the system, with no real end in sight.

TELEXFREE BUYS EXPENSIVE BED

TelexFree was a Massachusetts company, operating mostly in the United States and Brazil, founded in 2012, that sold Voice Over Internet Protocol (VOIP) phone service. The company was founded by Carlos Costa, Carlos Wanzeler, and James Merrill. The company would charge promoters' packages at sign up for $1,425 each. They would then earn money by posting and viewing advertisements on the Internet for the company. Most agree that no one ever posted ads, and those that were posted were never viewed.

TelexFree gave credits based on the ad postings and recruiting of new promoters. The company was operated as a classic Ponzi scheme, using the money from new investors to pay the credits for old investors. In April, 2014, TelexFree was shut down by the SEC and an action, both civil and criminal, was filed against the company as well as Costa, Wanzeler, and Merrill. Lawsuits were also filed in Brazil simultaneously.

During litigation, it was discovered that TelexFree had recruited in excess of 2 million promoters, with more than half of them in Brazil. The total funds that went through TelexFree were approximately $3 billion, and the money missing and owed was in excess of $1.8 billion. At the time of the shutdown, TelexFree had $5 billion in outstanding credits and only $100 million in assets available.

The case against Merrill proceeded smoothly when Merrill agreed to cooperate with authorities in exchange for leniency. He pled guilty and under a plea agreement was sentenced to six years in prison, and forfeiture of over $140 million in cash and assets. These funds will be used to refund promoters that lost money.

The case against Carlos Costa seems to have fizzled out in the U.S. He is a permanent resident and citizen of Brazil, and the authorities in the United States have left Brazil with the lead. His defense in the case is that the United States entity is to blame and that he just wanted to be the phone company in Brazil. His arguments have fallen on deaf ears. He has filed for bankruptcy twice, for reorganization, with both applications being denied.

The case against Carlos Wanzeler is the interesting one, he being a U.S. citizen who fled to Brazil to escape prosecution. Wanzeler left behind his wife in Massachusetts, with her claiming she knew nothing of the scam and was oblivious as to where the money was coming from, and that the couple was divorcing. Wanzeler kept insisting in Brazil that all the money was gone, spent on operations, and that there was nothing left.

In January, 2017, the Wanzeler portion of the case took on a new and fascinating spin. Law enforcement in Massachusetts had undertaken a sting operation in which they were monitoring Mrs. Wanzeler, not believing her claims of ignorance. She met with an individual one day, who was identified as Cleber Rocha. Mr. Rocha was followed and it was observed that he gave a suitcase to a cooperating witness containing $2.2 million in cash. Mr. Rocha was next followed to an apartment owned by the Wanzelers, where it was discovered they had hidden $20 million in cash inside the mattress. The money was meant to be transferred to Hong Kong, and from there routed to Brazil, where the estranged Mrs. Wanzeler was going to meet her husband to reconcile with him and the money.

In a case that may represent the most expensive bed ever seen, Wanzeler is still in Brazil a free man. The Brazilian authorities are refusing to cooperate with U.S. authorities in an extradition order.

AUTHOR'S FINAL THOUGHTS

I trust you have enjoyed reading these fascinating, if somewhat incredulous stories. They are just a small sampling of the financial scams that have happened throughout time. As you read this, there are many more happening right now, with unscrupulous individuals trying to separate you from your money. I have tried not to focus on any current scheme or scam, only those that have been adjudicated. I did not wish to stir up the defenders, something there will always be in every instance.

What I hope these examples have shown is that it does not matter what age, sex, nationality, color, religion, or economic status, you may still be a victim. You have seen victims from the working class struggling masses of third world countries to Presidents of the United States and captains of industry. Victims can easily be swayed by these crafty cons.

I have also shown that the scheme operators come from all walks of life, all nations, all races, creeds and colors. Indeed, they come from low social status, to the top of the social ladder. You have seen schemers that are 80-year-old women to young men. I have tried to expose you to scams run by paupers to schemes promoted by leaders of nations.

The only way for you to truly avoid being hurt in schemes and scams is to only invest what you can afford to lose and not put your money into anything that guarantees you a specific return on investment. Be cautious and careful when making financial decisions, and remember that all the common sense and careful planning may not prevent you from being taken advantage of.

All the best!

Scott Warren

ABOUT THE AUTHOR

An attorney in Southern California, Scott Warren has been practicing for the past 20 plus years with a specific emphasis on direct sales and network marketing. In his practice, he receives countless inquiries regarding various Ponzi schemes and other financial scams. He has represented both companies and individuals that have been the subject of investigations and victimization. He has spoken on stages, both big and small, in person and via media, on the dangers of "shady" investments and what to watch out for to avoid falling victim to illegal activities. Scott believes that you are your best defense in protecting your money and attempts to advise people accordingly.